Praise For The Auth

"Formula 1 for Business will give you the tools you need to get on the right track in your business and stay there. There aren't many authors who could assemble all the right information about laying the course and foundation for business success like Simon Frayne and Daniel O'Connor.

They not only help you get you started on a path to progress they help you identify your finish line in reaching your business goals and outcomes. Powerfully strategic, yet elegantly simple executable steps covered in this book will show you exactly how to turn your business into a vehicle for immediate and future success.

Over the years, I have read hundreds of books on business and business building and Formula 1 for Business rates near the top. It's a MUST read to turbocharge your business and accelerate your financial success. Get this book NOW--it's a game-changer."

Spike Humer
President of Spike Humer International, LLC
Co-author of "The 10 Day Turnaround"

"This is the most insightful, impacting & important book on building profit and value in your business you will ever read. It is a formula for success and is full of ideas, wisdom and strategies that can change your business forever. "

Darren J. Stephens
International Business Consultant and Bestselling Author

"Simon and Daniel have obviously put a lot of thought into the writing of this book. There are thousands of books out there on business but very few have the ability to encapsulate simple, easy to follow concepts that small business owners can put into practice to achieve very real results.

As they point out, most people in business today will want to exit their business at some stage in the future. And when they do – they will hope to realise a healthy profit for the fruits of their labour, often over many years.

In reality, very few ever go on to realise that dream. Following the advice and principles in this book, will go a long way towards achieving that goal. I would recommend any aspiring entrepreneur to read this book"

Peter Thorpe
Author - Small Business Street Smarts and former Editor – Australian Small Business Review

---

"Too often business leaders and entrepreneurs lack an objective framework so they can scale a successful business to the next level; this book provides helpful insights into just that and I particularly like the chapter on "Why it is better not to work in your business and how to manage your way out" as the paradox of good leadership is making yourself dispensable dramatically increases the value of the enterprise"

Andrew Banks
Chairman
Talent2 Ltd

'Formula 1 for Business is an outstanding breakthrough for 'Small Medium Enterprises' (SME's). By combining their sound business minds and vast business experience, authors Simon Frayne and Daniel O'Connor deliver a winning formula applicable to business owners small and large to achieve on-going financial growth, freedom from time in the business whilst allowing the business to grow into a valuable asset whose value can be realised through a future 'chosen' exit strategy. Straightforward and effective principles and practises that any aspiring or current business person would be foolish not to consider'...

Dean Gilchrist
Managing Director
SPORTSPRO

Life is getting faster. Everything about life is speeding up and more so in business. With their first ever book "F1 For Business". Daniel O'Connor and Simon Frayne have done to speed in Business growth, as Peter Drucker has done for management. They have presented it in a ready to use format, complete with the tools that go with it. If you are a business owner of any size or type, this has to be on your reading list …

Dr. Rajen Manicka
Chief Executive Officer
Holista Colltech Ltd

In a world of ever increasing time demands, it is refreshing when fundamental business concepts are delivered in a straightforward manner.

Formula 1 for Business is prepared for people within SME's by people who understand SME's – I commend it's reading to you.

Mark Collins
Managing Director
William Buck (WA) Pty Ltd

FORMULA 1
FOR BUSINESS

GLOBAL
PUBLISHING
G R O U P

Global Publishing Group
Australia • New Zealand • Singapore • America • London

FORMULA 1

FOR BUSINESS

A BREAKTHROUGH FORMULA
TO **DOUBLE YOUR PROFIT**
IN **10 MONTHS OR LESS**

Simon Frayne & Daniel O'Connor

First Edition 2013

National Library of Australia
Cataloguing-in-Publication entry:

Frayne, Simon, 1968-
Formula 1 For Business: A Breakthrough Formula To Double Your Profit In 10 Months or Less / Simon Frayne & Daniel O'Connor.

1st ed.
ISBN: 9781921630965 (pbk.)

Success in business.
Corporate profits.
Business planning.

Other Authors/Contributors:
O'Connor, Daniel, 1958-

650.1

Cover design and typeset by Global Publishing Group.

Published by Global Publishing Group
PO Box 517 Mt Evelyn, Victoria 3796 Australia
Email info@TheGlobalPublishingGroup.com

For Further information about orders:
Phone: +61 3 9736 1156 or Fax +61 3 8648 6871

Dedication

This book is dedicated to all the courageous, innovative, persistent, entrepreneurial, small to medium enterprise owners out there who have a vision and pursue it with passion. May your efforts benefit not just you and your family, but society at large.

ACKNOWLEDGEMENTS

We want to acknowledge our respective families for who they are and for providing continuous support on our life's journeys. Whatever the endeavour we feel very fortunate to know that they are always there for us.

Our inspiration for this book came from seeing the many small to medium sized businesses which do not perform to the level that they could or should and certainly not to the level which was envisioned when they starting out on their business journey. One business owner, a client, said to me after his business had been turned around into a very successful and valuable enterprise "why don't you write a book to help more business owners understand and apply the principles that turned me from struggling to thrive in my business and reclaiming my life". Thanks for the suggestion Ernie.

We would like to acknowledge the many courageous business people out there who seek to better their lot and maximise the value of their business for the benefit of their family and to society at large. We believe that it is these intrepid, entrepreneurial souls who crank the wheels of productivity in our capitalist machine. May you prosper!

We want to thank the many teachers we have encountered along the way, some during our academic educations, some as leaders in the corporate world, some formal mentors and of course the many people we have encountered who have provided valuable teachings from insight provided from their experiences. You know who you are.

To our many Formula 1 For Business associates whose commitment to our program has allowed for the rich contribution to many business successes, we thank you.

To our many, many clients who have placed their trust and belief in our program, teachings and integrity we extend special thanks; you represent our prime focus and it is through the rewarding interaction and work with you that we derive our greatest satisfaction.

A rich thank you to Cathy Jonas our Editor and to the fine people at Global publishing Group for the invaluable guidance, support and belief in our ability to transform our knowledge, passion and experiences in business into this book that we hope will help so many.

Of course a special mention has to go to you the reader. We acknowledge your desire to grow, improve, perform at a higher level and ultimately to fashion the business and life you envision.

Thank you all.

Bonus Offer

As a valued reader of our book we want you to have every chance of success so we are gifting you the following:

☑ 50% off membership to AIBO (Australia Institute of Business Owners) www.businessowners.org.au; as a finalist in their awards we have negotiated this special discount for readers

☑ Free video's which deliver a bite sized piece on specific topics designed to improve your business

☑ A free ticket to our next 1 day workshop seminar (valued at $97) which goes into greater depth on the business profit and value transformation concepts from the book

☑ A Gift Certificate of $700 to apply to our Business Diagnosis which provides a deep insight into the state of your business and is the first stage of our Formula 1 For Business Program; it costs $3,000, it value is much greater.

Go to www.formula1forbusiness.com now and enter your details along with the codeword 'supercharge' to activate your bonuses.

Table of Contents

INTRODUCTION

From a collective 40 years in business management consulting, this book was developed by two prominent Australian management consultants with the intention of awakening owners of small to medium enterprises (SME's) to the possibilities within their businesses. The writers believe even small business owners can have their business operating at increasing levels of profit and can build greater 'value' in the business so as to 'cash in' on the this value when they sell or use it to fund their life on an ongoing basis. The techniques and tips presented are commonly used by these and many other management consultants in medium sized companies, typically from the $10m to $50m turnover.

The need to take very seriously the challenge of making your business the best that it can possibly be is greater now than at any other point in history. This is the case (across western democracies) because we are fast approaching the time when Baby Boomers will be looking to exit their businesses to fund their retirement. In Australia there are 800,000 SME's and presently eighty percent of them are owned by Baby Boomers.

This means that within the next 12 years, 640,000 Baby Boomer businesses will soon be either 'on the market', passed down to offspring or simply closed down. It is clear that there will be a stampede of business sales, as well as a flood of 'exits' the likes of which we have never seen before. In this turbulent environment, if you intend to sell a business in the next twelve years you wil need to be very mindful of the level of competition there will be in the 'business sales' arena. You would be well advised to stand out from the stampeding herd of would-be sellers. This book is focused on helping the smart business owner make his business asset as profitable, valuable and attractive as possible in order to do just that.

It's likely that you are presently in the driver's seat of your business; and from the cockpit it seems that the world revolves around you. This is one of the factors that holds many SME's back. If your business is relying on you, you have a 'job' not a business. One of the key concepts of this book is to 'fire yourself' from the hands-on 'driving' and ascend to 'Team Management'; in Formula 1 racing not one team manager 'manages' from behind the wheel.

Many business owners who do not address the key 'pillars' on which business value is built will be left with a business in which no buyer is interested. You may have spent twenty years in building it up and may have been counting on the business to augment your ebbing superannuation accounts and real estate portfolio, to provide surety and security in what should be your golden years. This is the real potential tragedy looming for many SME owners right across the western world, but it can be averted with the right perspective, planning and action.

The good news is that there are always buyers for good businesses. The operative word here of course is 'good'. In the eyes of the prospective buyer, that which makes a business more valuable and more 'saleable' will also make it more profitable and will provide the owner with more time and lifestyle. So whether you are seeking to renovate a business specifically for sale or are looking to maximise the performance of a business without a foreseeable sale, the information contained in the pages to come will deliver the foundations for your success.

One of the key principals underlying the philosophy of this book is that 'if you are not growing you are going', which is to say that 'if your business is not expanding faster than CPI, you are losing the value, profitability and ultimately you may lose your lifestyle. Statistics bear out that if an SME is the same size (revenue and profitability) and it was twelve months ago, it actually has less than a fifty percent chance of breaking even in three years. This suggests that there would be little perceived value in the business, which goes against the very reason we are in business.

But 'growing' is not confined simply to revenue and profitability, these are the end results. These end results are reflected by growth in the forms of 'improvement' and 'evolution' within the various functional aspects of the business. If you are not always improving you are effectively 'standing still', while all those across the competitive landscape in which you play are improving and moving forward, the reality is that you are really 'going backwards'; and often at a more alarming rate than thought possible, particularly now when the rate of change is greater than ever.

The authors have consulted to many businesses over the past 25 years and have distilled a structured 'Formula' to help determined business owners to success. When applied, this 'Formula' serves to multiply profitability and tangible business value. The process will provide the means by which to improve profitability and the value of your business but also 'how' to go about working your way out of the business, for maximum payback. 'Formula 1 For Business' uses as a metaphor for business a Formula 1 racing team which has many of the same components:

The Vehicle is the business itself and naturally much attention needs to be placed on the set up, capacity, functional efficiency and speed at which the vehicle performs. Without a fast and reliable vehicle you simply cannot win in either in the competitive area of the F1 racetrack or in the competitive arena of business. Our focus is firstly to do the things which will allow the vehicle to get up to full speed.

The Driver is critical because no matter how impressive the vehicles performance capacity, it simply will not perform to capacity if it is not driven with skill and expertise. If the driver is only accustomed to driving at a speed of a hundred kilometres per hour and yet the vehicle can deliver two hundred kilometre per hour performance, the vehicle will not deliver it's potential. This can often be the case with small to medium enterprises so we also focus on the skill and comfort zone of the person driving the business.

The Pit Crew are other team members are the staff. Without attracting, motivating, getting the best out of and 'keeping' the best staff, it is very difficult for the vehicle to reach anywhere near optimal performance. Pit crew performance either in F1 racing or in business can determine success or failure and we invest some time in showing what works in having employees perform.

Specialist Engineers are represented by those specialist advisors that provide council to the business to comply with regulations and enhance performance. Accountants, Lawyers, IT specialist, HR specialists and Management Consultants all contribute to strategy, various aspects of operations and ultimately play a huge role in overall success or failure.

Information Monitoring is crucial to both the race car environment and the ability to run a business. You can only manage what you can measure and having accurate and timely information and measures in business today is the basis for sound decision making. Knowing the KPI (key performance indicator) measures of a business and the people within it largely determines the performance of the vehicle. We provide the seldom discussed insight into 'knowing your numbers'.

The Sponsors are those who provide the financial backing for the whole venture. They seek to gain a return from their investment from a winning team. Both business and racing would be impossible were it not for the 'sponsors'. In an SME this may be the owner, the bank or even some outside interest; their performance imperatives must be satisfied. Attracting or building the finance for your venture is critical.

The Fans are the stakeholders and buyers of your product or service and without their following, contribution and satisfaction the show cannot go on. Ultimately there must be a market for the product or service, someone willing to purchase. Acquiring a customer and keeping them is the basis for business growth and ultimately what determines your business success.

All of these components are necessary, functional contributors to the ultimate function, profitability and value of your business vehicle. Throughout the book we provide insight into the various components, how you can make them work for you and what to do to enhance their role in building your businesses profitability and value.

Another key concept within 'Formula 1 For Business' is that of 'incremental improvement.' Elite performance in any field is a function of many small improvements and constant vigilance with monitoring. The system we present will help you to implement one thing at a time and to be diligent in testing and measuring everything you do.

The book does not provide any quick-fix or window dressing, temporary or illusory benefits. The experience of the authors is that when most business owners get started with these tools, they eventually fall in love with their business all over again. They typically enjoy substantially greater earnings, often for significantly less personal effort and ultimately build the value of the business which can be 'cashed in'.

This book is not intended as simply a nice read to while away your precious time but rather as an instructive device to improve your lot. Also don't expect everything to work the first time you try as rarely does success come in the first effort with anything – you need to persist.

We have witnessed this transformation happen to all sorts of businesses and their business owners and it is our sincere hope that when you implement several of the techniques in this book, you will enjoy the transformation from hard-working operators, to manager, to owner to business collector/trader.

We wish you well in your quest to transform your average family wagon enterprise into a Formula 1 racing business!

Are you ready? Is your harness secure? Now, start your engines.....

CHAPTER 1
'The Formula' – Starting the Season with a Competitive Race Machine

"Formula for success: rise early, work hard, strike oil."

John Paul Getty

CHAPTER 1

INTRODUCTION TO THE FORMULA 1 PROCESS

Sadly, modern-day businesses get started, operate and all-too-often die, for all the wrong reasons. We have observed businesses that have floundered and in some cases died, when they could have (and in some cases should have) been spectacular success stories. We have also seen competent business owners and operators who have been forced to sell their businesses for little or no reward, for all the years of hard work they dedicated to the cause. We have also seen highly qualified owners with business degrees, who bought and subsequently killed good businesses, and in nearly all of the above cases the principals always had somebody or something to blame.

If, right now, you are standing in an airport bookshop, casually thumbing through this book to get one gem, or "secret" to keep your business growing and ultimately reward you with a passive income until you decide to accept a favourable offer from a keen buyer, then I will give you the first of many - up front. Businesses fail because people fail. Circumstances around us are constantly changing and it is up to us as the drivers of dynamic businesses, to adapt our business operations to the changing landscape. If we don't change our business model to match the new buyer demand, we can face extinction and if we are not mindful, it can happen quite rapidly.

But why do university graduates also fail? There may be many reasons for this, but for me (as a post-graduate with a partial doctorate in process) I put it down to the difference between knowledge and know-how. Most commerce and economics texts are filled with superb examples of knowledge but in most cases, academics can't teach you know-how. I know that most consulting academics will argue that they have business experience running their own (usually one-man) practices and/or their departments, but how many of them have faced the real hardship of a market paradigm shift (if you want to understand this, talk to the owner of a video rental store) or a legislative barrier? Think of those people who started or purchased an LPG changeover business for vehicles in Australia, before the government started to talk about abolishing tariff subsidies on LPG, or the installation subsidy on fitting gas to a vehicle.

This book focuses on business know-how, for a practical learning process that can be understood and used by anybody who has or wants to own a business. Most importantly, the knowledge can easily be implemented by the reader without too much effort. I urge you, the reader, to absorb one chapter at a time and implement the knowledge as you go. It requires care to ensure the business you have does not experience too much turbulence at once, as staff and customers can both become disillusioned and seek to distance themselves from the business.

Let me firstly present my key reasons for why academically qualified business owners may not be able to perform better than any other owner. It is my firm opinion that the value of a tertiary education does not lie in the content. You don't go to university for knowledge. You go to develop the tools of learning. Yes, you have to learn how to analyse knowledge and also how to store it in sufficient quantities to regurgitate it in exams but most of the knowledge you gather is dated from the day you graduate. If you fail to recognise the value that lies in your tools of learning, you will stop learning when you finish your studies and you will immediately start to lose the competitive advantage you have as a graduate.

I have been very passionate about having graduates I work with understand that these tools of learning are not unique to universities. Many business owners develop their own tools of learning and if they continue their learning journey by exercising these tools, they will overtake any graduate who believes his or her parchment is the proof that they know it all now.

If you are still reading this, you are perhaps not a closed-minded graduate and accept the merit in a constant-learning model of continual education. If so, let this book become your first set of practical lessons, with easy-to-implement action steps that we use in our Formula 1 business coaching program in order to double business net earnings in 10 months (and 56 steps) if the program is understood, implemented, measured and embedded.

Preparing for Race Day

Could any of the Formula 1 drivers of today, have started their careers in F1 vehicles? Certainly not! They would need to develop advanced skills and competencies to even make it to the racetrack and then some serious wins in smaller (less complicated) classes would eventually identify the most skilled and elite drivers for selection into the big-time.

So it is with business. We don't jump into a major corporation at our first attempt. We need to learn the business rules as they apply to the industry and the markets that we seek and we then need to turn some of our knowledge into know-how. Most of us do this as employees, working our way to management within someone else's company, making mistakes and learning along the way.

Ultimately, when we have our experience and we are ready to fulfil the dream of owning our own business and being the boss, we have to learn a whole new set of rules. It may be that you have never had to balance your cash daily or calculate the turnover and/or projections for the lenders before.

In most cases, the new layers of learning are harder to grasp than the operational functions and we struggle to bring it all together. If, for any reason, we choose to focus on getting the operations running smoothly, we are not maximizing our resources. As the business owner, you need to start with the end in mind and the end game is to have more competent operators operating the business, while you manage it. This means you need to allocate some of your valuable time to the practice of management, to get you away from the operations as quickly as possible. To best achieve this we recommend an eight-stage model, which is detailed in this book, as a practice model for most small businesses. These steps are:

Segment the operational functions. Even if your business has a part-time workforce of one, you still need to plan it out as if the fully-operational full-scale business is inevitable. You need to prepare the organisational chart for the firm and then start to create the divisions or departments. Typically, these would be around (1) Management and Administration, (2) Finance and Accounting, (3) Production/Service and R & D, (4) Human Resources and (5) Marketing and Sales. Although these may be broken down further in major corporations, they are still structured around these five key functions.

Identify the positions. Typically, the organisation chart may have a manager in each of these positions, with your name under each, from the commencement. The art of true growth is to get the names of other quality employees on these functions, as quickly as possible.

Set the operational function for each position. After the organisation chart has been set and you can fully document the functions within each position, you then need to draft up the job description. Although you will be performing most of the tasks in the short-term, you will need this experience as part of the knowledge-base you hand on to the incumbent in the induction process.

Work out the accountability for each position. Each role will need a job description and position on the organisation chart, clearly identifying the role, to whom they report and also who reports to them. This structure ensures full accountability from the end of induction.

Set about hiring someone for each position, against the job description you set. As you expand your business (based upon your hard work and strategic planning brilliance) you follow the basic recruitment process for selection, appointment and induction, with you sharing your experience in that position, with the incumbent. The recruitment process for all positions identified may take several months or even years, but with the right paperwork in place and the procedures for everyone to follow, you will not have to go back and repeat the process when people leave.

Work with each person until they are comfortable and competent. Some small businesses consider the induction process to be a half-day exercise and will view it as lost productivity for the position leader. There is considerable research available that bears out the theory that the more comprehensive the induction process, the more likely the candidate will engage and become part of your team. The temptation for most small business owners is to focus on business and see induction as a cost (lost business) but the long-term strategic business manager knows the value of hiring once. Don't be tempted to drop employees in deep water but be ready for their inevitable mistakes during the learning process.

Measure the individual and collective operational performance. As your first employee becomes part of a growing team, the KPI measures you put in place will enable you to remotely monitor and measure your business and not have you work in an operational role to grow the business. It is essential to give regular feedback to teams and individuals, so that corrective action can help all employees adjust to their roles and functions.

Focus on the outside. Once you have the business in a strong and steady growth trajectory, you can now begin to look outside the company. Your focus now switches from growth through operational efficiencies, to growth from other areas. These areas may include new customers, offer more products or services, new regulations, opportunities, compliances, suppliers and contractors, as well as protecting your intellectual property and know-how.

Once you are out of the business (with no operational functions) your very presence and your access to accountabilities (KPIs, etc) will ensure the business will continue. With encouragement and with regular adjustment against the KPI trends, your business should prosper, if the outside environment remains the same.

Your final role is to look for your next business. Could this be a business you buy from or supply to? Could it be a competitor? Could it be a new branch in another area, as your first attempt to prove your business model as a franchise?

Why Change Anything?

In consulting, one of the first sessions we have with business owners (before accepting them into a change program) is to have the business owners set their outcomes. To effect this managed change, we provide

100 points for them to allocate on their goal priorities. We offer them the chance to invest in any proportion, in the following outcomes:

- Increasing the net earnings

- Reducing the hours worked by the business owner, and

- Increasing the sale value of the business, as a going concern.

The most immediate response from business owners is to affirm their desire to double their net earnings. Forcing business owners to decide how much of this as a priority they would be willing to trade-off, in order to effect gains in one or both of the other areas, can be confronting for any of them. This may be the first time they have been encouraged to think about these other options, as part of their overall vision for the business future. The intent becomes even more pronounced when they discuss the trade-off with a business partner and/or spouse.

People understand that with the scarcity of resources, they could not achieve increases in all three areas of their business operations within a ten month period, unless they employed several full-time consultants. They would also need to be willing to entertain an extended period of turbulence, as the business is dissected and re-built from different directions.

From the very beginning of the change journey, the business owner should feel confronted by their own personal goals and making these congruent with their business goals. The goal-setting process (for personal or business applications) will almost always start with the vision and include a mission and a stated set of values. These personal VMVs are then measured against the business VMVs to ensure congruence. If there is a difference (and there usually is) this is the first change requirement that we would work on, in their business model.

The underlying messages and themes that we are going to share with you in this book are packaged and presented in understandable and implementable nuggets. The intent is to deliver each of these practical and proven business concepts in "bite-sized pieces" for you to recognise, understand, implement and measure, before returning for another. Some of the core concepts we need to embed within our business practice, include:

- We need to measure everything we do, so that we can improve it

- We need to focus on one area at a time and not change too much at once

- We need to make incremental changes not massive changes

- We need to implement strategies that will ensure we are not working in the business

- We need to structure the operations which will make our business most attractive to buyers and will deliver us the highest value at sale

- We need to Increase our margins by adjusting our profit drivers (so the value increase is less about pricing), and

- We focus on fixed and variable costs, supplies, channels and potential partnerships, to enhance and extend our outcome-activity ratio.

What Can Go Wrong?

In most cases, business owners have had some exposure to business consulting or coaching, with little or mixed results. In a lot of cases, this may have less to do with the programs and more to do with the turbulence or confusion it can create in an uncontrolled change interval.

The temptation (particularly when you have just acquired a business) is to make a list of changes you would like to implement and then rush into changing them all at once. The result for most businesses is turbulence. Employees do not perform at their peak if everything around them is being changed, including the rules they work by and the accountabilities with which they are measured.

The three key principals for managing organisational or operational change in any organisation is (1) To keep change to minor, incremental changes over time, changing one area at a time if possible, (2) To have a change interval, followed by a period of consolidation (to embed the changes), before looking to implement another change interval, and (3) Communicate the intent to all team members and explain what outcomes you are trying to achieve. These three simple rules will help your changes to be received positively and to become standard operational procedures within a much shorter time.

Once you have set up your structure and prepared your growth and change program, you are ready to build your racing business vehicle to be competitive in the races you enter and ultimately, to be dominant in your industry.

What Happens When your Business Accelerates?

This book is presented as an easy-to-read operators guide for small high-growth businesses, but as you continue to understand the process, you will begin to see this as far more. Once you have completed a diagnostic review of your current business, ensured the processes are documented, the kinks ironed out, the tweaks implemented and the improvements measured and proven, you will find that your own role will transition from operator, to driver, to owner and later to the entrepreneur. At present, you might be working hard in your business and looking for a way to reduce your working hours without reducing your income.

One of the most common first reactions that business owners have to the suggestion that they need to be out of their business, is "My business can't do without me." This is all too common thinking, for managers as well as the thinking some business owners have for key personnel. In most cases, there is no foundation to this thinking.

In August of 2011, Apple announced that their charismatic leader and chief innovator was stepping down for health reasons. Analysts predicted a share price plunge, from its then present position of $368. As we know, Steve Jobs died a month or two later but some 12 months after his death, the shares were trading at $624. If such a pivotal key person can make such a small difference in his exit, in one of the largest companies in the world, what impact do you really think your exit would have?

The longer-term objective for us as authors and management consultants is to have you hone the skills of assessing, buying, building and either selling businesses or building a portfolio of cashflow businesses that can provide you with far greater returns than property or equities in publically listed mature companies.

Somewhere along this continuum you are going to choose to stop your journey and this could become your "comfort-zone" for months, years or even decades. We are hoping you revisit this book when you become restless and continue your journey to entrepreneur and develop your E-factor to the point where you collect cashflow companies like properties in a game of monopoly.

SUMMARY POINTS

☑ Even if you are a company of one, you need to have an organisation chart.

☑ You should plan the positions, their roles, responsibilities and accountabilities, before you hire.

☑ You may wear most of the management and operational hats today, but you must start to plan the recruitment process to give these roles to competent people.

☑ All roles must be clearly defined and measurable. People need to understand how you will judge their performance as good or bad.

☑ When all positions are allocated, you are only looking at the measurable areas as performance monitoring tools.

CHAPTER 2
'The Dream' – Vision, Mission, and Values

"Those with a vision flourish and those without a vision perish"

Dr John Demartini
(Modern day Philosopher)

CHAPTER 2
'THE DREAM' – VISION, MISSION, AND VALUES

Vision, mission, and values are the foundation on which great efforts in organisation are built. Whether in the competitive arena of the racetrack, on the fast-paced business racetrack or some other human group effort, these three elements are critical in driving your collective resources towards a successful outcome.

It is all too commonly the case that owners and managers of small to medium enterprises (SME's) dismiss the significance of vision, mission, and values as mere 'fluff' when considering the future plans of their organisation. Seldom in fact do we find an appropriate level of focus and commitment directed towards these things when embarking on a commercial venture and this may be one of the key factors in the low level of success in the world of the SME. After all, it is difficult to succeed on a journey for which there is no clear destination (vision), no stated 'reason to be' (Mission), and no set of rules to govern behaviour and decisions (values).

Each of these form an integral to the success of any business or group effort whether or not they are boldly and formerly stated or subtly communicated and understood through commitment to action.

All great journeys, projects, and endeavours begin with a vision. Initially this may take the form of a vague and nebulous dream but long before there is any consideration of planning for action there is always considerable time and energy devoted to refining this dream into a clear and distinct set of possibilities; a vision.

If you have a drivers licence you may be a car enthusiast. If so, your vision of you as a driver most probably started before primary school. Most boys dream of driving a car long before they are old enough to own one. They may start with a toy car or tricycle and graduate to a go-kart. I still recall the very first time I was able to slip into the driver's seat of a car and turn the wheel while I pumped away at the pedals.

There was no risk of me setting this car in motion, as it was without wheels (and possibly an engine) in my Uncle's back yard. I can still recall the smell of leather and the shine of the chrome strip across the top of the dash that joined the glove box to the single dial on the driver's side. For that brief moment, I was in charge and I could go anywhere…

A business vision is a seductive image of an ideal future, one that is seen clearly enough to be articulated in a form which will provide inspiration and motivation to all those who are willing to share it and accompany the leader on the journey towards attaining it. Every great person and business that started with a vision has provided real excitement and passion because their vision represented a 'destination'; it establishes clearly, where they were headed by answering the question 'where are we going?'

Steve Jobs revealed his vision of technology's future to Inc. Magazine in 1989 (after famously being fired from his own company in 1985) in an interview. He spoke about "the big insight", as he called it, that he and others had had in the 1970's regarding the importance of putting computers into the possession of regular folk. He believed in the enormous creative capacity of individuals - if given the right tools. He proposed, "a thousand people with microcomputers will always outperform one person with a supercomputer" and that "because people are inherently creative, they will use tools in ways the toolmakers never thought possible, and then they will share what they've learned". This revealed an extraordinarily accurate vision of the future for personal computing.

In 1997, the year when Jobs returned to Apple, at the World Developers Conference he said "We've tried to come up with a strategy and vision for Apple--it started with: 'What incredible benefits can we give the customer?' and did not start with: 'Let's sit down with the engineers, and figure out what awesome technology we have and then figure out how to market that.'" Going right back to the 1970's, and 80's Steve Jobs has had a rich vision for the future which has actually shaped what is now the present, where individuals enjoy the benefits of tools which Apple pioneered. Jobs always had a strong response to the 'where are we going?' question and there are thousands of followers who would love to have the opportunity to work with him and share his vision of the future.

For organizations like Steve Job's Apple, having a vision and communicating it to the team provides the focus, energy, enthusiasm and commitment to get things done; the right things. Because it is necessary, firstly to have a clear vision of the desired destination before it is possible to plot a course to get there. Far too many organisations undertake the challenge of developing strategy and planning before they have crystallized their vision. 'What exactly are we looking to achieve?' The answer to this central question will go a long way to determining 'how' to go about the work necessary to getting there.

Taking off on a journey without a precise understanding of where you are going is a futile exercise; like getting in your car and just 'driving' without knowing where you are going, you will waste valuable time and fuel, and worse still you will likely become deflated for your lack of a satisfying outcome. This analogy may sound a little silly but this is exactly what many business owners do when embarking on what is one of the most serious and significant endeavours in their life: running a business.

However, having a vision is not just the domain of world changers like Steve Jobs and Apple. Everyone is business needs a vision to fuel the fires of direction and activity. Even if only a relatively small concern, having a vision in business usually determines the difference between measured success and mediocrity.

A friend of mine in Bunbury, Western Australia, has a cleaning business and her vision when starting out, was to have it run under management providing her with a specific income and freeing her time to do other things. Having that focus on a vision which is meaningful to her has allowed her to achieve it within record time and now she holds the privileged position of being able to spend her time how she wants and can expand the vision to even greater heights.

A Harvard university study concluded that we need vision for three main reasons:

- To clearly perceive what is possible: To focus on a vision is to consider the possibilities and to reach for an inspired future. Once the desired possibility is perceived, recognising the details allows for the formation of a clear vision, which will in turn allow for the development of strategy and goals.

- To overcome the drift effect: With vision comes purpose; without a vision we lack purpose and we tend to drift aimlessly. Vision is critical to overcome this 'drift effect'.

- Because having a vision is the key to creating effective change: To effect positive change in any field it is necessary to focus on the 'desired outcome'; the clearer the vision of the person or the business, the greater the success that entity will experience.

If you do not have a vision for your business, you are on a journey without a destination akin to a rudderless ship and you will wander aimlessly looking for answers only to return to what you already know. I remember an old saying that goes something like: 'when you not aiming at anything you hit nothing a hundred percent of the time'. Having a clear vision is the first step towards being able to identify the targets you are 'shooting at'.

Many business owners are so short-sighted because their focus is on doing 'urgent' things and as a result, they can hardly see past tomorrow.

Urgent versus Important

We have seen so many businesses which simply do not have a clear vision and it is a prime contributor to their eventual and inevitable struggles. Many people who have come from having a job (even those from lofty corporate positions) to driving the wheels of entrepreneurialism fail to recognise the importance of clearly defining their vision and then fall prey to the 'urgent' things at the expense of the 'important' things.

When you really look, the urgent things are rarely the important things and the important things are often not urgent. The seemingly urgent things such as emails, phone calls, customer needs, and administration can all be streamlined or delegated. However, the important things like dedicating time to refining your vision and building strategy to define how to achieve the vision will never be done if you do not make them priority and schedule time for them; time, that is uninterrupted and nonnegotiable. When all said and done there is nothing more important than having a clear vision so allocate time to building and maintaining it.

When you think of 'visionary' people, it is natural to conjure up images of great folk such as Bill Gates, revolutionising the significance of the personal computer, or Henry Ford, who envisioned a world where everyone would want one of those newfangled mechanical buggies (and people though he was insane!), or Richard Branson, who continues to extend the Virgin brand across countless industries. However, 'vision' belongs to us all. We were all designed to create our own possibilities and 'business' provides the ultimate platform to achieve our dreams.

The people referred to above are well known for building an organisation around their vision, which provided the driving force for the business to flourish and prosper. They all dedicated significant time and energy to conjuring a detailed vision which would define their organisation, they spent time on strategy and they were quick to employ capable people to deliver much of the urgent operational requirements.

The great business leaders ensure that they are not held hostage to 'unimportant urgent' and reserve adequate time for the very important 'big picture' things; vision is the most critical of these 'big picture' things.

This does not just apply to captains of industry; the same applies to leaders of successful small businesses. We should not be lured by the executive position in large corporate companies. There are many more small business owners and builders who make far more money than if they took senior positions in large corporate organisations. They have several distinct advantages in their business operations, including their freedom to dream, to take holidays, and to change almost anything without being accountable to shareholders and auditors.

Partnering up with success

A small business client in the northern suburbs of Perth has long since reached his financial saturation. This is where he could not hope to spend all of his wealth in this lifetime and quips he will have to rely on relatives to get rid of it all for him. He has (at last count) more than 15 businesses in which he has a significant share, but in nearly all of these (apart from his real estate agency, his property rental roll and his business brokerage) he is willing to share this with other business leaders, provided that their vision and integrity matches his.

He makes his business partners feel uneasy about where they presently are heading and want to shift to a higher level of activity, profit, market share, etc.… Most of his partners come to him for money to finance their small business operations, but end up with something far greater than just an increase in profits. Darrell has a way of building their vision to a point where they understand they were aiming too low. In nearly every case, their gift of equity to him still gives then a greater company value than they would have had if they achieved what they set out to do and he eventually owns a chunk of their enterprise that still represents more than they originally had in most cases.

Most of us have heard the story of the senior QANTAS exec who commissioned feasibility on a low-cost airline. Although the numbers all worked, his bosses killed off the idea so they did not dilute their brand. He recognized the opportunity and sought a partner with vision. He found one in Richard Branson and Virgin Blue was born.

Your Personal Vision

It is important before developing a clear business vision however to be clear about your personal vision. It is critical that your personal vision is congruent with the business vision because your drive to pursue the business vision will be dictated largely by your personal reasons for wanting business success.

It always fascinates me that many people will dedicate more time and energy to envisioning and planning for a three week annual overseas holiday than they will to their own life. They ream over the details to ensure that everything goes absolutely smoothly for those three weeks only to abandon themselves to 'the urgent' when they return from holiday. Sit down and really consider what you want from a personal perspective and what you 'don't want', and make sure you document this; something magical happens in the subconscious when things are documented that allows for your desires to come about.

Once you have determined, detailed and documented your personal vision you will be far better situated to see your business vision clearly in a way which will ensure that your these two respective visions are congruent.

Your Business Vision – Starting With The End In Mind

We have all heard the statement 'start with the end in mind'. This is the very essence of developing a vision, as it demands that we understand in detail the outcome that we are aspiring to achieve. We need to define our destination.

When setting about the task of determining your business vision it is best to start brainstorming and capture everything that comes to mind in terms of 'what we want to be'. Pretend that you have already achieved your vision and see with clarity the specific details that make the vision and capture these details in documentation. The more specific and clear you are in this process the better.

Try answering the following questions to provide some shape and form to your vision:

- What does the business look like?

- What is its size (revenue, profit, staff, geography)?

- What is the business known for?

- How do we measure our success?

- Why are we important?

- What don't we do?

- What is the working culture? (how do employees feels about the business?)

- What solutions do we provide to solve what problems for our customers?

- What is my role? (owner's roles?)

- What do customers, employees, industry peers and the community say about the business?

The better you can answer the questions above the greater clarity you have for your business vision. By definition, your vision must be five years out or beyond and must be a stretch that represents real growth and evolution and serves all stakeholders.

In many ways, your vision of who you will become is one of your greatest assets. This is so because it defines how you identify yourself as a business; your business identity. How you see yourself will determine your conduct, your alliances and the level of game that you play as an organisation, it will contribute to your mission and will determine your values.

Once you have clarified your vision and it has becomes real, its value also becomes tangible in the sense that you can actually trade on it. For example, in recruiting the best staff, in negotiating with preferred suppliers and vendors and even in acquiring key customers a vision, which resonates, can have a positive impact that starts the relationship off on the right foot.

Clarity Brings Focus and bringing detail to your vision is the key factor behind being able to identify strategic objectives so developing a full and coloured vision is critical in ultimately developing action plans to step your way to success. You vision identifies what success means.

Vision Statements

A vision statement is just the tip of the iceberg breaching the ocean of possibility as it often represents a far greater and deeper vision than can be expressed in a condensed statement, which is typically a paragraph long. Many business owners misunderstand and underestimate the significance of a vision statement as 'just words' when these particular words represent the desired future and destination for the organisation in question.

A company's vision statement should play a central role in driving the business forward from both the internal perspective of uniting and focusing those who are charged with the responsibility of delivering in the company's name and the external perspective of boldly stating to the world at large what the ultimate objective is.

However, the true power of a vision is not so much in the wording itself, but in how much your vision truly reflects the aspirations of your organisations stakeholders (owners, employees, client's) and how much it is embodies in your whole organisation. This means that the vision needs to be shared and owned by those who are responsible for delivering it, your employees. Share your vision statement with every new employee and ensure that it resides in a prominent place where existing employees can be reminded of it. It is one of the best ways of having staff 'sing from the same song sheet' in recognising that they are all working for a common cause.

Here are some examples of vision statements:

"Democratise the automobile"... Ford in the early 1900's

"To become the world's leading Consumer Company for automotive products and services"... Ford more recently

"A personal computer in every home running Microsoft software"... Microsoft

"To be the number one athletic company in the world"... Nike today

"Crush Adidas"... Nike in the 1960's

It must be said that some people easily often confuse 'Mission' statements with a 'Vision' statements. For example when conducting research I founds that many websites out there claim that Nike's vision is: "To bring inspiration and innovation to every athlete in the World", however this is clearly a 'Mission'. Always remember that a vision statement is by definition something that you want to become, something you want to achieve, an alluring picture of a beautiful future – whereas a Mission statement is about why an organisation exists, defining its purpose (we will talk more about this soon).

When your vision becomes clear and a greater focus than your past, your future becomes more valuable than your past and great things begin to happen. Make the time to focus on your vision, create it into a detailed picture, and savour all the details. Do this and you will be rewarded a hundred fold more, than simply doing the work that your business does.

Mission

As referred to briefly above 'Mission' is all about explaining the 'purpose' for the business and defines 'why we exist'. Unlike 'Vision' which is focused on the future look, shape and feel of an organisation, 'Mission' defines what a business is here to 'do' in the here and now.

In defining your company's 'Mission', you should be answering the following questions:

- Why does the business exist?
- Who is our customer?
- What are we committed to providing to our customers?
- What promises are we making to customers?
- What is our Unique Selling Proposition?
- What wants, needs, desires, pains and problems do our products / services solve?

Mission statements are typically a paragraph long and certainly no longer than a page. They require time, thought and planning to really get to the heart of why the company exists. Most people discover that the process of developing the mission statement is as beneficial as the final statement itself. Going through the process will assist you is specifying the reason for what you are doing and clarify the motivations behind your business.

Some Tips For Developing Your Mission Statement

Involve those connected to your business. It helps to get the views of other people in seeing the strengths, weaknesses, and pitfalls you might miss. Make sure that you choose positive, supportive people who want to see you succeed.

Set aside time to develop your Mission statement. Even though the statement itself does not consist of many words, there is depth behind it, which requires exploration. It takes time to capture in words the organization's heart and soul, which acts as a reference point to everyone, involved in the business.

Brainstorm. Throw down everything irrespective of how silly it might sound. After having exhausted all ideas then rationalise them to collate statement, which get to the purpose and then work on refining.

Use "rich descriptive words." After you have captured the essence of what you are trying to communicate in your mission statement, continue to craft and polish it until it is the most vibrant and colourful expression of your purpose; after all this is what you are putting 'out there' to the world as to why the business exists.

Following are some Mission statement for high profile organisations:

"To produce high-quality, low cost, easy to use products that incorporate high technology for the individual. We are proving that high technology does not have to be intimidating for non-computer experts." ...Apple in 1984

"To enable people and businesses throughout the world to realize their full potential'.... Microsoft today

"The purpose of the Cooper Tire & Rubber Company is to earn money for its shareholders and increase the value of their investment. We will do that through growing the company, controlling assets and properly structuring the balance sheet, thereby increasing EPS, cash flow, and return on invested capital"...... Cooper Tyres

"We fulfil dreams through the experience of motorcycling, by providing to motorcyclists and to the general public an expanding line of motorcycles and branded products and services in selected market segments"..... Harley Davidson

Mission statements are clearly important in providing direction and formalising purpose for a business organisation but they are underpinned by 'Values'.

Values

The values of an organisation represent what is most meaningful to it and sets the 'intent' for the business. Values help identify commitment to standards and act as a compass for determining behaviour and conduct within an organisation, both between colleagues 'in house' and in front of customers and the 'outside world'. Put simply they represent what your organisation 'stands for' and 'believes in'.

As with Vision, values can sadly be dismissed as mere 'puffery' by some less than switched on business drivers. The truth is that Values actually set the standard for conduct across a business and reminds owners and senior staff of how to set the example and be congruent. As an example, if an organisation has as one of its key value 'respect', then shouting at a peer or making snide, underhand remarks would be far from upholding this value. People can easily sense incongruent behaviour, which at worst will be seen as hypocrisy so it is critical once values have been identified that these values are upheld in every exchange and transaction that takes place.

It is easy to see values in action throughout the recruitment process when statements are made about the organisation and enquiries are made of candidates to understand whether he or she shares the same values. This is one of the reasons why it is far better to be overt and quite clear about what the business values are. There can be no room for ambiguity when it comes to values. Values must be stated.

Values are a serious matter and must be genuine; they must be 'lived up to' by those who create them otherwise there will be a credibility crisis in the eyes of the employees who are supposed to live by them. There is nothing worse than the boss who preaches respect, demands respect and yet does not exhibit any. Values are a wonderful opportunity lost to many organisations because they are either not set with enough thought or are not made to be part of the daily affairs of the business.

For some clever business owners, Values have become real business drivers and played an important part in helping the organisation stand out. Take for example Virgin Blue Airlines who's values are 'Resourcefulness', 'Innovation', 'Caring', ' Enthusiasm', 'Excellence', 'Individuality' and 'Integrity'. Serial entrepreneur Sir Richard Branson has instilled these values into the organisation from the top down and they clearly play a central role not only in 'hiring', but provide guidance in all-important decision-making and direction. The business has clearly benefited by taking some of the market share of main rival Qantas.

After having clearly identified, documented and communicated your business values, be sure to highlight, recognise and encourage behaviour which upholds and promotes the values. Make sure your business values are clear to employees so they can live up to them and emulate the best.

If you show them the way and give them a chance, you will discover that they can be your greatest advocate.

Clearly identifying the vision, mission, and values for your business provides the necessary foundation upon which to build a successful organisation. In racing terms, they are like visualising the championship, knowing the rules, and defining the team philosophy. Only after these foundations have been laid is the competitive unit in a position to develop strategy and plans for achieving victory.

So how much of a visionary were you as a child? How much of this has been educated out of you and how much of it has actually survived layers and perhaps decades of management? Can you reach into your mind and put a spark into that "dreamer" that used to come up with ideas all the time? How hard can it be to get in touch with that creative child within us all? That dreamer may just put you well ahead of where you are aiming for, all because nobody told that child not to dare...

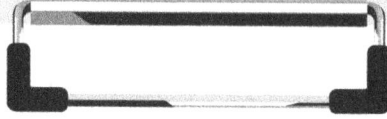

SUMMARY POINTS

☑ Vision is the foundation upon which success and greatness is built.

☑ Vision is critical for direction, strategy and to bring staff along for the journey

☑ It is important to focus on the 'Important' things and delegate the 'Urgent' things in order to be successful in forming and pursuing vision

☑ Ensure that your personal vision and business vision are congruent.

☑ Start with the end in mind.

☑ Your Mission is all about 'purpose' – why the business exists

☑ Values are the basis for behaviour and conduct

CHAPTER 3
The Formula for Victories – Strategic Planning

"The one sure way to success is to know everything you can about what you do."

Donald Trump

CHAPTER 3
THE FORMULA FOR VICTORIES
– STRATEGIC PLANNING

So, you have developed a rich and exciting vision for the business, you have identified its mission or 'purpose' and you have formed the values by which you wish the business to be run. What's next? The next critical phase in reinventing your successful business from the ground up involves developing strategic plans to connect your mission and your present state of play to your vision of where you ultimately want to be.

The common sense way to go about strategic planning dictates that you first understand 'where you are now' before determining 'where you want to be' and then formulating a plan as to 'how you should get there.' The funny thing about common sense though, is that it's not too common!

Too often, people leap into planning how they intend to achieve certain outcomes without first having a clear understanding of exactly where it is that they presently sit with their business. This is very much like having a road directory to plot a course to a specified destination without knowing what your present location is. You may as well not even have the map because without knowing where you are now, you are lost.

Where Are We Now?

When presenting to groups of business owners, we frequently use an exercise to help people understand the importance of understanding their current status. We get them to cover their eyes with their left hands and then with their right hands, we ask them to point NORTH. We then invite them to open their eyes and look around, while still pointing. There is always a wide variance as to where north is.

We then ask, "If I was to ask this group to relocate to a point north of here, how many of you would be able to talk to each other after you move? How many would need to shout? How many would need a phone or a flag to signal the others?" This exercise will generally help people to understand that they need to know where they are now, what they have now and who or what has influenced that, before they start to plan how to get to where they need to be.

Business Diagnosis is the first stage of the strategic planning process and is geared towards identifying this present 'state of play.' Just like when you're setting the performance expectations for a racing car, it is first necessary to have a detailed 'look under the bonnet' before it is possible to determine what needs to be done to get it up to top performance.

When seeking to answer the question, 'Where are we now?' it helps to consider the external environment and the internal environment. The external environment consists of the business environment, the industry, the competition, technology, customers and shareholder circumstances. These, by their 'external' nature affect the business but are outside the realm of our influence. Each of these elements however, provides critical insight into how the business should be structured and function to give it the best chance of success. For example, industry benchmarks and competitive analysis provides valuable perspectives on how those operating in the industry function and give markers on what works and what does not. Good sources of industry analysis are the Australian Bureau Of Statistics, Australian Institute of Export, Chambers of Commerce and industry peak bodies. Some general competitive analysis can be acquired through these groups however, more specific competitive analysis may require engaging a marketing firm.

The internal environment consists of the strategic elements of vision, strategy, structure and culture together with the functional elements of products and services, marketing and sales, people, systems and processes and finance. Unlike the external environment, all these internal elements are subject to our direct control and therefore should undergo a greater level of scrutiny and thought.

Business Model

When considering strategic planning, it is necessary to define your 'business model' which is basically answering the question: How are you going to make money? Behind this basic question is a bunch of other more detailed questions such as:

- Who is your target customer?
- What problems or challenges do you solve for your customer?
- What value do you deliver? Are there 'added value' opportunities?
- How do you connect with, acquire and keep customers?
- How do you define and differentiate your offering?
- How do you generate revenue?
- What's your cost structure?
- What's your profit margin?
- How do customers pay?

It all starts and finishes with the customer. Defining who the customer is and what you do for him is the cornerstone of any business. The more you know the customer and understand his or her particular challenges and difficulties the better able you are to satisfy them; so really get inside the mind of your customer and try to see life from their perspective.

How you go about generating revenue is a function determined by who the customer is and how they value what you are offering. For example, if you are selling luxury sports cars, you are delivering value beyond simply the functionality of that vehicle. You are providing the feeling, the excitement and the status that goes with owning such a vehicle. This will influence the way you form connections with your customers and the tactics involved in shifting them from interested party to customer and then maintaining them as a long term advocate.

Of course, in order to make profits as important as generating revenue in your business model is, your cost structure and your profit margins are critical. Many wise business people make 'margins' one of their primary focuses. Having a constant and vigilant outlook on margins means that cost structures are always under consideration and maintaining margins means maintaining profits given a constant volume of work and increasing margins means increasing profits. Increasing or at least maintaining your volume of work is largely related to your ability to communicate your competitive advantage or how well differentiated you are.

Competitive Advantage

To get a clear understanding of where the business is at present and before developing a coherent strategy it is critical to define your competitive advantage. This is essentially what you are best at and what your organisation can potentially do better than other organisations within your competitive landscape.

A competitive advantage is in play whenever a business is able to deliver the same benefits as its competitors at a lower cost (cost advantage) or deliver greater benefits than competing products or services (differentiation advantage). So, competitive advantage provides for greater value being delivered to the customer and greater profits being derived by the business.

Competitive advantages can exist where an organisation has greater skills and know how than its competitors, though this is not usually a long term, sustainable scenario as competitors develop the same skills. Or competitive advantage may be the result of a strategic partnership with a large industry player which affords the small firm buying discounts, expertise and the benefit of technology and research and development.

A competitive advantage may be the result of being the 'first mover' where you are first to bring something to the market, usually disruptive technologies (like the iPhone), or it may simply be the result of 'location' in the case of retail businesses like restaurants, petrol stations and retail shops.

One of the greatest competitive advantages comes in the form of 'intellectual property'; that is Patents, Trade secrets, Trademarks and Copyrights. The strength of these lies in their legal protection and enforceability; nobody else can do what you are doing exactly the way you are doing it. This is the greatest and potentially most valuable differentiator.

Whatever your competitive advantage, it is critical that it is clearly articulated as it forms the basis of what message you take to the market and how you are able to create value for your customer. If you haven't yet built your competitive advantage you need to get to it now; it is the foundation of your business.

SWOT Analysis

Another important tool in determining 'where am I now' is the SWOT analysis (Strengths, Weaknesses, Opportunities and Threats). Assessing your firm's strengths, weaknesses, market opportunities, and threats is quite a simple process that can offer powerful insight into the potential and critical issues confronting your business.

The SWOT analysis begins by identifying all the internal strengths and weaknesses in your organisation. You will then determine the external opportunities and threats that apply to the business based on your market and the overall environment. Don't be too concerned about building huge detail into these at first; bullet points are the best way to begin, as what's important is to capture the factors you believe are relevant in each of the four categories. The primary purpose of the SWOT analysis is to identify and assign each significant factor, positive and negative, to one of the four categories, allowing you to get an overall perspective on your business. The SWOT analysis will be a useful tool in developing your goals and eventually building your marketing strategy.

It might be helpful when conducting an analysis of your strengths and weaknesses to consider the functional elements of the business separately to ensure that you cover everything. Namely: Products and Services, Marketing and Sales, Human Resources, Systems and Processes and Finance. Remember to be objective and that the more accurately you identify these four elements, the more valuable the SWOT will be for assessing where the business Is placed and in building your plans for the future.

Also remember that 'opportunities' (and 'threats') are external factors that reflect the potential you can realise through implementing your marketing strategies. Opportunities may come about because of market growth, lifestyle changes, solving problems associated with present conditions, market perceptions about your business, or the ability to offer greater value that will build demand for your products or services. It might be relevant to place timeframes around opportunities. Ask yourself if it represents an ongoing opportunity, or if it is a window of opportunity. How critical is your timing?

The implications of the SWOT analysis are significant because when the internal strengths and weaknesses are compared to the external opportunities and threats, there is real insight into the condition and potential of the business. Ask yourself how you can use the strengths to take advantage of the opportunities on offer and how can you minimise the harm that threats may cause if they materialise. How can weaknesses be reduced or removed altogether? The real value of the SWOT analysis is in bringing this information together, to assess the most promising opportunities and the most crucial issues so that you are able to build sound plans.

The Perceptual Map

A Perceptual Map is a tool which is used to assess where those who are in charge of a business think the business is positioned in terms of whether they should 'shore up,' 'selectively expand,' 'aggressively develop,' 'acquire,' 'diversify,' 'defend' or 'exit.' Their responses to a series of questions are put into a computer program which will determine if their 'perceived' position is in alignment with their 'actual' position.

Actual And Perceived Strategic Position

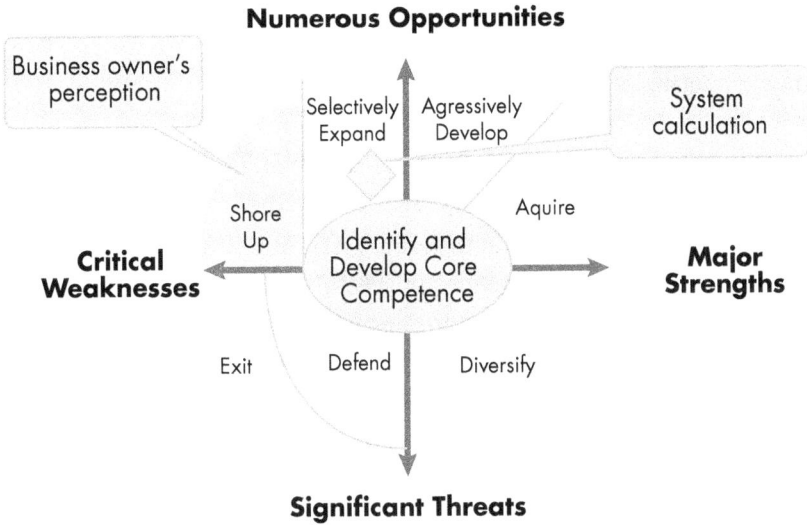

Numerous Opportunities

Business owner's perception

Selectively Expand | Agressively Develop

System calculation

Shore Up

Aquire

Critical Weaknesses

Identify and Develop Core Competence

Major Strengths

Exit | Defend | Diversify

Significant Threats

Even without the software required to calculate your actual position, it is a valuable exercise to give some serious consideration to where on this map your business would be positioned, given an understanding of competitive advantage and the findings from the SWOT analysis. The relative positioning on this map will influence your strategic objectives, the strategy you adopt and the goals that need to be achieved along the way.

Where Do We Want To Be?

Short Term and Mid Term Focus

Having determined where the business is currently situated by answering the question, 'Where are we now?' it is possible to begin considering a response to the question which asks, 'Where do we want to be?' In order to develop some specific objectives, milestones and measures to assist in the journey towards vision it makes sense to identify where we want to be at specific intervals which represent the short term and the medium term.

A sensible short term time frame is six months, while three years represents a reasonable mid-term time range to plan towards. Six months is a good short term time frame because it is long enough to implement some significant improvements and yet it is short enough to be able to connect the objectives to monthly and even weekly goals and activities. Looking too far beyond three years is generally a difficult thing to do given the increasing rate of change that the business landscape is undergoing.

First, determine where you want to be three years from now and from there develop a more specific focus for the six month time frame. Below is an example of 'where we want to be' across these two time frames for a client of ours, (a professional services firm):

Specifically, In 3 Years:

- Be recognised as one of the major regional consulting firms in the state
- Have a number of regional offices
- A choice for directors to be 'what proportion' operational
- Be doing projects of choice (targeting projects we want)
- Attracting the best talent

Specifically, In 6 Months:

- Conveyed vision and values (present in actions)
- Roles, KPI's and expectations and development paths of staff established
- Key staff acquired
- Business development program developed and commenced
- To be in a position of understanding to decide 'where,' 'when,' 'who,' 'what' and 'how' to open the initial regional office

The objectives for the first six months are clear and certainly provide a focus for more detailed planning and for activity in the short term while the objectives for three years provide a broader perspective which is heading towards vision. It is important that there is a connection between short and medium term goals which is meaningful to those driving the development of the business.

Strategic Objectives

Strategic objectives are continuous, long term areas of focus which will move the business from performing its mission in the present towards achieving its vision. Ask, 'What are the key areas of focus and associated specific outcomes which when achieved in the medium term will have us on the way to attaining the vision?'

Strategic objectives will apply through both the six-month and three-year imperatives and beyond as they represent a link between the present and the envisioned future. Below are the strategic objectives for the business referred to in the above section where three year and six month targets were identified.

Strategic Objectives:

- Be able to acquire/attract the best staff
- Develop regional presence
- Actively grow the business with marketing and sales
- Achieve financial targets
- Staff development, recognition reward, satisfaction and retention
- Implement service expansion

Of course it is important to understand whether or not you are on the right track during the course of time and for this reason it is critical to have a number of goals for each strategic objective. Below are the goals associated with the first strategic objective above (Be able to acquire/attract the best staff):

Goals:

- Determine forecast level of demand for new staff in each discipline in accord with business development program (Measure: Have staff requirements plotted looking three years ahead)
- Identify immediate and intermediate staffing needs (Measure: Identify immediate staffing needs)
- Develop a unique value proposition to potential staff for acquisition (clear benefits) (Measure: Unique value proposition established)
- Develop processes for staff acquisition (avenues) (Measure: Search and recruitment processes established)

- Acquire required staff (Measure: Key positions being filled within two to six weeks of recognised need)

Once goals have been established for each strategic objective and you have effectively identified the 'what,' you are in a position to develop strategies for 'how' you are going to achieve the objective and the goals along the way.

How Should We Get There?

When asking the question, 'How?' we are entering the domain of strategy and action. At the broadest level 'strategy' is matching organisational strengths with market opportunities to provide value to the customer, or the target market. This represents a key element of the Business Model and should be revisited at least on a quarterly basis to ensure that it is still appropriate.

For each strategic objective (the 'what' we want to achieve) there will be a strategy (the 'how' we will achieve it). Strategy may be stated in as simple terms as an answer to the question, 'How are we going to do that?'

For example, in the case referred to above where our first strategic objective is to, 'Be able to acquire/attract the best staff,' the strategy stating how we will achieve this is broadly stated as:

Strategy:

- "Become more attractive to the best staff in the industry and become more aggressive in our pursuit of the best staff."

Goals and Action:

Goal: Determine forecast level of demand for new staff in each discipline in accord with business development program (Measure: Have staff requirements plotted looking three years ahead)

Action: Develop a view of mid-term (three years) staffing requirements for each division in the context of aggressive business development program

Action: Plot the evolution of the organisational chart over the next three years

Action: Identify the point at which new staff will be required

Goal: Identify immediate and intermediate staffing needs (Measure: Identify immediate staffing needs)

Action: Examine the organisational structure of positions required

Action: Develop a set of 'ideal' staff characteristics/personal attributes

Action: Develop detailed job descriptions (with performance measurements) for new roles

Goal: Develop a unique value proposition of potential staff for acquisition (clear benefits) (Measure: Unique value proposition established)

Action: Share vision and value with staff (* do this for all existing staff at the outset)

Action: Identify attributes that make our business a great place to work (and will make it so in the future)

Action: Develop a USP (Unique Selling Proposition) for staff

Goal: Develop processes for staff acquisition (avenues) (Measure: Proven successful process established)

Action: Identify and document ALL the means of acquiring staff

Action: Establish a preference for the respective means of acquiring staff

Action: Identify the stages/steps within the various ways of acquiring staff

Action: Build a process for staff acquisition

Goal: Acquire required staff (Measure: Key positions being filled within six weeks of recognised need)

Action: Make our environment and offering attractive for potential staff

Action: Implement process for staff acquisition

In following this process you will have as a result, an 'Action Plan.' Of course, goals should have timing requirements attached to them (much more on goals in the next chapter) and as a result you will likely have different sets of actions associated with your various goals. Then you are able to group actions into different chronological steps which will form the basis of your Phased Action Plan.

What Have I Got to Help Me Get There?

Throughout the strategic planning process it is necessary to be mindful of what resources you will need to attain your objectives relative to the resources you have. Resources may take the form of capital, people, plant and machinery, premises, alliances, intellectual property or even time and it is critical that you have a sound grasp on the resource requirements behind your ambitions.

It is a well-known truth that many businesses starting out, tend to underestimate the amount of financial resources or capital required to promote the success of their business so plan your financial needs in detail. Recruitment and development of the people can also be a critical factor, given that the nature of many modern businesses is based on the skills of key people. It is important that there is a documented summary of skills your team have, relative to the collective skills you will need to pursue the strategic objectives and ultimately the vision of the business.

Always be mindful of the resource requirements when planning to achieve your sought after objectives and assuming that your resources are 'finite,' you will most likely need to make some important decisions about how you allocate those resources. It is a useful first exercise to allocate an imaginary 100 units of each resource (say time or capital) and assign these units across your Strategic Business Units or projects over a given period of time (say a year) to get a grasp on the proportionate allocation of the given resource. Then do more detailed calculations of the specific quantity of resources necessary to deliver your plan.

What Do I Keep and What Do I Throw Away?

Another key consideration throughout the strategic planning process is an analysis of what you should keep and what you should throw away. This may apply equally to products and services, clients, staff and processes and is an important part of living the reality that a business is always evolving and never stands still.

I have seen many instances where a business has persisted in providing a product or a service simply on the basis that they have always provided it in the past despite this product or service yielding very little profit or worse still at a loss. It is important to look at this practice from the perspective of 'resource allocation' as resources invested in an unproductive activity, section or project represent opportunity costs for the more profitable activities (and the business) in that: were those resources invested in the more profitable activities, the business profits more as a result. Of course there are instances where a service may be a 'loss leader' to a larger, more profitable service but these things can be done with a strategy in mind rather than simply tolerating underperforming offerings.

For example, I know a printing and design business which makes healthy profits from its printing and design operations; it provides a prompt, efficient, well priced service with good customer service. It carries a retail stationery shop because the business, which has run over a number of decades, has always offered stationery however, the shop makes less and less money.

With large national stationery warehouses (such as Officeworks) and other large office supply franchises who have massive purchasing power, this business simply cannot compete for price or range so customers buy elsewhere for their office supplies and stationery needs. The downside of this situation is that the resources required to run this shop (people, floor space, money and time), if diverted to the printing and design operations, would provide a far greater return to the business (and of course the owners).

It is often useful to clearly define 'core' versus 'non-core' activities in a business to understand in no uncertain terms what the prime focus of the business is and where the priorities lie. This reduces the temptation to get caught up in peripheral activities and issues referred to in the previous paragraph and make sure your focus is where it should be – where you want the business to be in the near future.

How Will I Know If I Am There and If I Am On The Right Track?

The key to knowing if you are on the right track and when you have arrived at your desired destination is having specific goals which you can measure and which have a clear 'achievement point'. Measurement is one of the foundation concepts in this book and it underpins all successful businesses. Trying the 'manage' without 'measurement' option is an exercise in futility.

It is important to have a number of key measures which provide insight into the overall progression (or otherwise) towards the key objectives of the business and its mission. These are often referred to as Critical Success Factors which are really the few key areas where things must go right for the business to succeed and if performance in these areas is inadequate then the overall performance of the business will be similarly lacking.

When determining your Critical Success Factors, you must ask yourself, for each strategic objective, "What business activity is essential to achieve this objective?" The answers to these questions are your potential critical success factors. Then you will need to analyse this list of potential factors to identify the essential elements of success and these become your critical success factors. Decide how you will monitor and measure them, communicate them with your team and then ensure that you develop an automated system to monitor and measure.

Now this needs to be an ongoing process, not a 'once in a blue moon' event. The strategic planning process itself may be an annual focus however, there should be quarterly strategic updates to determine how progress is going. Every quarter, questions should be asked like, "Have we hit our targets this quarter? What did we do well? What did we do poorly? What did we learn this quarter?" and, "How can we do better?"

Regular reviews will ensure that the plan is still relevant for the competitive landscape and circumstances that the business operates in. It is a little like a race car going in to a pit stop for assessment and recalibration. Decisions and adjustments to strategy can be made on the basis of strong measurement and monitoring disciplines and everyone in the team can be realigned to the plan. In our Formula 1 program, we insist on monthly Project Status Reviews with all of the members, to ensure we hold them to account on all of the agreed tasks and we measure the progress of change and the benefits achieved at outcome. We are able to plot the progress and accurately predict at month three, who will not achieve their core objective (double their EBITDA in ten months). This is critical for us, as we provide a money-back guarantee and we need to know who is not implementing their customised program as we have all agreed.

Your strategic plan does not need to be an enormous document, on the contrary, the more streamlined and to the point it is, the more effective it is likely to be. Remember, this is the primary document from which the business is driven so it demands the utmost of your quality attention and the input of your key people. Know that you can drive your business vehicle with a great deal more speed, precision and confidence when it has been set up properly with the right strategy.

With the right understanding of 'where you are' and the right strategy to get you to 'where you want to be,' you have a better-than-even chance of being more than competitive out on the business racetrack.

SUMMARY POINTS

☑ Strategic planning is essential, but a strategic plan should not be a long and tedious document.

☑ Start with an assessment of current resources. Where are you and what have you got to date?

☑ Clearly define where you want to be at the end of the planning period.

☑ What needs to be done to get to where you plan to be?

☑ Who will do what to help you get there?

☑ Review of internal and external issues that could affect your plan.

☑ How will you measure your progress in achieving each objective?

☑ What resources will you use/need to implement this plan?

CHAPTER 4

Driver Training
– Goal-setting &
Monitoring

*"Obstacles are those frightful things you
see when you take your eyes off your goal"*

Henry Ford

CHAPTER 4
DRIVER TRAINING – GOAL-SETTING & MONITORING

You have just woken up with a very strong headache. Your brain feels a bit fuzzy as you look around you to try and get your bearings. You quickly realize you were not sleeping – you are alone in the front seat of your vehicle and you have been in a significant road accident. From what you can see, the situation has been devastating to your vehicle, but as you get your senses back, you realize you are uninjured! You turn off the ignition and slowly step out of the car. As your "shock" starts to clear, you realize your vehicle has been totally and completely destroyed, but you are uninjured… What you choose to do next, will most certainly define your future.

Let's consider the road you are on the "highway of life" and the accident one of the many situations we face in business or family life, as we continue our journey. In some cases, it may be bad planning, bad choices, or just bad luck that creates situations such as these. You may know people who have more than their fair share of bad luck, but the following might help to explain this for you.

The responses to a life-changing situation like this can be generalized into three categories. The first is wallowing, where one might sit on the side of the "highway" and accept sympathy from passers-by, who in turn admire your luck and empathize with your loss (the vehicle was surely an asset). Some people can allow incidents in their lives to stall their journey and these become an excuse for them not to re-start their journey. The most significant item they lack is hope. This response can sometimes be referred to as grieving or despair. There is no reason we should deny ourselves these feelings, but we should always seek to set an end to this period and set off to find that highway again.

The second response could be exodus, where you feel compelled to get as far away from the crash site and the memories as you can, both physically and mentally, causing you to set off to anywhere that is "somewhere else". This may provide you with immediate relief from the bad memories and allow you not to face any fall-out or have to explain to others what you do not want to recall. This is sometimes referred to as denial or avoidance. I am not advocating the denial of this option, but simply expressing the need to limit the length of this phase.

The third response is the reset. This is where you reassess your situation, work out how you can get yourself back onto that highway and before you set off, you make a quick assessment of the vehicle for any items that may be able to assist you (in that analogy, house-keys, wallet, first aid kit, insurance papers, etc., may prove handy later). This is regarded as the entrepreneur response. It is very rare that you will find anybody that has survived more than a decade in business, who has not faced a serious incident on his or her respective business or personal highway. The entrepreneurs simply re-set their lives and start back onto the highway of life. Their business may be a total disaster, but they understand that seeking professional help or having the business humanely "put-down" may give them some residual tools or assets, but also will clear their focus for the continuation of their journey.

These two most important tools required that will always set the entrepreneur apart from the other two categories, is Hope and Goal-Setting. The former is not considered a topic for this book, but we will now focus on how structured goal-setting can keep a business, a team or an individual, moving forward on their journey, helping you to shift from the breakdown lane to the fast lane, as your focus shifts from the immediate incidents and disasters, to the planning and achievement of the future vision of your business and ultimately, your life.

One of the grandfathers of the personal development industry, Paul J Myer (back in 1961) said that 'the single most powerful effect on human motivation comes from goals'. This is because even if you make only a humble stride towards a big goal, the fact is that you are moving in the right direction. This 'positive feedback' is very significant in that it has a powerful effect on increasing your motivation to continue and dedicate more resources to pursuing and attaining that goal, as what you have done so far is paying dividends.

Most people lack sufficient motivation to do great things, chase their vision (if they have one), or really pursue the life they want simply because they lack clearly defined goals. After you have clearly defined your vision, your goals will come into better focus because they will have meaning and context for you.

In addition, the best part is that once you have recognized that you are moving in the right direction and your motivation (and belief) is engaged, the strides towards your goals become greater and greater until your momentum carries you towards your desired outcome with enormous speed and efficiency. When you dedicate time to goal-setting and goal action you will find yourself achieving your goals and living with a new level of invigoration.

Goal-setting is widely acknowledged as a central factor of success in any field of endeavour but it applies more to the business field than most other pursuits because of the number of factors contributing to success, failure or simple mediocrity. Because business can be a complex game, it is critical that time and energy is devoted to proper planning and goal-setting so that everyone involved has real targets to shoot at.

We have all heard the old cliché 'if you fail to plan, then you are planning to fail' together with that ripping old chestnut 'when you are shooting at nothing, you hit the target every time' and yet we see far too few people and businesses take planning their goals seriously enough.

I have observed people planning a three week holiday trip overseas and the level of detail and purpose involved was impressive. The irony was though that these very same people do not devote nearly the level of energy, detail, or purpose to planning and goal setting for either their lives or their business. It is little wonder that their holiday was an escape to paradise after which they returned to the ramshackle mediocrity of their usual life and underperforming business. Setting goals for yourself and your business is important and will largely dictate where you end up.

Defining Your Goals

The development of your goals comes from the detail and clarity of your vision; from the big picture of where you eventually want to be, distil down the various pieces of your vision, which may be addressed as a goal. In order to qualify as 'A Goal', these pieces of your grand vision puzzle must have certain qualities, they must be S.M.A.R.T:

SPECIFIC: Goals need to be specific so that you know when you have achieved them, the more specific the better. For example 'I want more money' is far too vague to be a goal, whereas 'I want $100,000 extra cash from my business by June 30th' is specific. Without being specific, you are chasing the wind. Jack Canfield (personal success author) said in his book 'The Success Principles' that 'vague goals produce value results'. You need to make your goals as detailed as possible in order to achieve the specific outcome that you want.

MEASURABLE: Goals need to be measurable not only to tell when you have attained them but how you are progressing towards them while in pursuit. You may have heard a little saying that I love: 'YOU CAN'T MANAGE WHAT YOU CAN'T MEASURE'. This is so true and very important from a motivation perspective because if you cannot discern whether you are moving towards your goals or simply spinning your wheels you are likely to abandon them. This can lead you feeling flatter than if you had of 'failed'; at least failure is feedback that you can analyse.

ATTAINABLE: It is very important from a motivation stand-point that goals are attainable. If a goal is not realistically obtainable then you will not actually go after it with full force and vigour; your subconscious will chip in with 'why bother putting in the effort if I am not going to make it'. This point also goes to breaking goals down into actionable steps and clear milestones so that your goals are not perceived as 'too big'; it's critical to have wins along the way to keep you going.

RELEVANT: This may sound as obvious as the nose on your face but goals need to be relevant and relative to your purpose; congruent with your vision. Time is your most precious resource so you cannot afford to waste a minute in pursuing goals which do not contribute to your greater vision and purpose. Always ask the question 'will this serve my purpose and vision?'

TIME BOUND: You must have a deadline when setting goals. If you do not have a 'target date, what you have is a 'dream' not a goal. Time imperatives have a magical influence on your getting things done, conversely if you have no target date the task just tends to drift on forever until you tire of getting nowhere and drop it. I'm not sure who said 'if you want something done assign it to a busy person' but there is truth in this, people getting things done tend to get things done to a schedule.

Now these 'qualifiers' are usually referred to when addressing personal goals however they are equally applicable to setting business goals. In fact, when you introduce the additional dimension of a number of other people to the equation of goals setting and planning it is even more critical that these qualifications are observed to ensure that your team can really identify with the goals and own them themselves.

Aligning Your Goals

When defining goals, you must have alignment between your personal goals and your business goals (driver and vehicle); after all, the reason you are in business is to serve your life's aspirations and live the life of your dreams – right? Your personal goals and business goals must be congruent; they must both be corresponding puzzle pieces that fit together in your life's grand vision puzzle.

For example, if you have a personal goal to spend time with your young children and savour their 'growing up' years (hopefully that's not until 30!) and yet you are presently the 'Driver' in your business vehicle which demands fifty hours of your time in the business per week, there is no real potential of alignment here. Clearly, something has to give and some serious decisions will need to be made. Ultimately, your business is there to feed your life, however the business needs to be up to speed and functioning efficiently to do this. Where you are in your business maturity cycle will determine your ability to hand the 'driving' to someone else; well aligned short, medium and long term goals are all required to do this and to fill your visions 'puzzle'.

There is another perspective on alignment, which is about aligning the respective business goals and personal goals. You need to get the chronological order and priority level right with the various goals that contribute to your bigger picture. If it is necessary to first organize the key personnel in your business in order that you can be confident of delivering satisfaction to customers with your 'operations' then you don't want to go out and implement your aggressive Marketing and Sales program before your capacity to deliver is well on the way to being in place. You are likely to have a number of goals at any one time so ensure that you prioritize and order them accordingly.

The ultimate alignment for goal-setting is to have your team members individual goals aligned to your business goals. If this can be achieved, you will never have to measure or motivate your staff again. In companies where the energy levels are up and the staff members are all happy and cooperative, you will almost always find shared goals or aligned goals. This creates your corporate or team culture and will inevitably bid a team for a longer term.

Individual/corporate goal alignment is not an easy objective to achieve in its own right. You must first accept that there are two methods of making this a reality in your company. The first is in hiring, where your interview questions determine the goals and aspirations of the applicants to compare and contrast with yours and those of both the team and the company. These second thing is to set these goal alignments individually (one-on-one) with the team members, so that they can build personal ownership in these goals.

A colleague of mine tells of a powerful example of goal alignment in a printing company in the USA. They had a very experienced senior sales person who was not achieving his full potential and they wanted to get him back to his peak performance. His outward appearance was still cheerful and encouraging to the regular sales team members, but he had clearly "lost his edge."

The consultant casually interviewed him in his car, as they drove from customer to customer, in a normal working day. They talked about everything from family, management, competitors, and future and the one key issue for this person was his company car. His competitor, working for a similar company across town, had the luxury version of the car he was driving and this senior sales executive made the off-hand comment that "parking that in the client's car park was always going to show them he was more important and therefore, give him the edge". (not his words). Discussions of bonuses and promotions did not have the same resonance as this small issue.

When the implementation phase was commenced, the consultant recommended that the company set a pathway for sales achievement that would upgrade this senior sales executive's vehicle to a model above the competitor's model, with a short-term method of his "earning-in" this reward, through an average performance on three months, for his agreed 2-year sales and profit objective.

This vehicle was earned and delivered (on a promise of consistent achievement on agreed sales performance) after three months and the performance goals were now completely congruent with the organization goals. The Rep was very happy, everyone around him benefited from his sense of achievement and positive energy and the company did not have to suffer poor performance figures or worry about replacing perfectly good personnel.

Goals Need To Be Written

This brings us to one of the central aspects of setting goals and planning for success: 'documenting them'. Don't think that just because your goals are 'important' that you will always remember them and dedicate the necessary time and energy required for them to deliver. Goals need to be WRITTEN down and if they are not you are really kidding yourself.

Most people write a shopping list because without it they forget the important things and are lured in by impulse buying. The same principle applies when pursuing your goals; unless you keep yourself focused on what is important, it is easy to be knocked off course and, worse case, get lost in meaningless and superfluous distractions. When goals are written and you revisit them regularly (preferably daily) you stay locked onto your target and are likely to hit the bullseye that is achieving them.

There is another reason to write goals down. Something magical happens in the subconscious mind with regard to the 'how' when goals are fed into the conscious mind in the written form on a consistent basis. After regularly revisiting written goals, your subconscious mind will begin to accept the new goals and incorporate them not as "change" but as the optimal course of action. To retrain the subconscious, we can use several techniques, including 'spaced repetition', which essentially has the desired goal repeated to the subconscious on a regular basis (a bit like radio advertisements) until we can sing it like a jingle. The other successful method, is the use of multi-sensory input, which requires that we read, write and hear the goals into our conscience mind, so that our subconscious will resist it less if it is familiar with the goal or action.

Your ability to focus on the required outcome is so much more powerful when goals are written and regularly reviewed. As a young man, I was a cricketer. I was in the Western Australian Sheffield Shield squad as a 20 year old as an aggressively, egomaniac top order batsman. I always used to diligently record my results in writing: How many runs I made, how I perished (mode of dismissal), my running average, and aggregate for the season. However, up until the age of 27 I never set 'performance goals' for the season. That year I set for myself goals to make 800 runs, make a double hundred and average more average 50. An amazing thing happened: by being focused on some targets, half way into the season I had already made 550 runs and had on one day blistered a sensational 215 (dismissed just after tea). Setting goals had focused me in to performing at another level; of course I should have been doing this far earlier in my playing days!

So documenting goals is clearly important when setting personal goals, however it is even more important when dealing with team goals because everyone needs to have the same interpretation of 'what we are looking to achieve' and 'how we are going to do it'. I find it mind blowing that some business owners who do not document 'what we are looking to achieve' and the specific goals and measures required to get them there, actually expect that others in their team (responsible for delivering) will have the same understanding of what is requires as they do. Not only are there no agreed upon imperatives, but there is no 'map' by which to tell whether they are on the right track or are about to fly off the track and possibly be trapped amongst the burning wreckage.

Documented goals and plans to achieve them are critical in business; all stakeholders need to be able to focus on what is required and revisit the objectives regularly against the measures set to understand precisely how they are performing against the plan. When goals are identified and plans mapped out to achieve them, this is the 'beginning' of the process not the end; many make the mistake of putting together plans only to neglect them. Once plans are agreed upon, they need to be regularly referred to like a map in navigation to stay on track.

Some other key Elements to Goalsetting and Planning

Benefits to be gained & losses to be avoided – 'The WHY?" When setting goals and drafting plans it is important early in the process to identify the 'why'. It has often been said that when you have a big enough 'why' the 'how' will present itself. In terms that are more specific, this can be identified by 'benefits to be gained and losses to be avoided'.

As an example, if you are looking achieve a goal to lose seven kilograms and the plan to achieve this is to do the necessary training to run a half marathon (without stopping), the reason you have, 'the Why' of losing the weight and being a new, lithe, more attractive version of yourself (and all the associated benefits), is the big reason to keep you training. Without a big enough 'why' to remind yourself of to keep you going during the challenging times, you may fall prey to your old habits and lose sight of the reason you set the goal in the first place.

Obstacles and Solution: At the point of documenting your goals it is wise to identify possible obstacles that may emerge to stand in the way of your achieving them and doing some brainstorming around how to overcome these obstacles. This is best done is an uninhibited brainstorm session where you get everything down onto paper which may get in your way of achieving the goal.

Once you have exhausted all your ideas as to what could possibly get in your way in achieving your desired goal, and then list all of these obstacles, with some space between each one on the left hand side of a page. Then come up with possible 'solutions' for each obstacle, the more the better. This is a really valuable exercise in that the forethought given to obstacles means that if and when they emerge, they have less power to thwart you and present you with far less stress as you have already developed a solution. If you brainstormed enough on obstacles then you should have a ready prepared list of solutions to refer to get you past any problem that can impede you in your progress towards your goal.

Action Steps and Milestones: Another key element to efficiently achieving goals is to break the goal down into a number of smaller 'action steps' considering each a 'milestone'. Personal development guru Anthony Robbins calls this 'chunking' and it simply refers to identifying smaller pieces of a goal so that the goal is more digestible in small increments and gives you cause to celebrate milestones along the way in recognition that you are moving towards your goal.

Often people become atrophied when they consider what it is that they have to do as 'too big', will take 'too long' and they will have to do 'too much' to achieve it. This is why it is so important to break goals down into action steps, each as a milestone. We need to regularly receive feedback that we are achieving movement in the right direction and as long as we do, we are motivated to continue taking action.

Sharing Intent: We have all done it; made a commitment to ourselves and then because nobody else is there to keep us honest with ourselves we can shirk it and wriggle out of the responsibility. The classic situation where you say to yourself 'I will get up tomorrow at 5.45 and go running' and when 5.45 comes and it is dark and cold, just you around and no one will know if you don't go. This is the reason that real goals are shared with someone you respect who will keep you accountable.

This is one of the main reasons why people have a 'training partner'; even the most disciplined sometimes need help keeping honest with themselves and pushing their boundaries. Not following through on your plans also has a very destructive impact on your self-esteem and your belief in your ability to follow through; conversely, every time you DO follow through your planned actions, your belief in yourself becomes stronger, and your momentum grows.

The Importance of Measurability

It is worth mentioning again the importance of 'measurability' in achieving your goals. 'YOU CANNOT MANAGE WHAT YOU CANNOT MEASURE' is a mantra by which you should approach your goal-setting. It is best to have simple measures, which allow you to clearly understand whether you are winning or losing in your goal quest.

For the person looking to run a half marathon to lose weight may have measures around action such as 'run 6 kilometres, four times per week without stopping' and 'alter lunch time dining menu from my usual two meat pies to two chicken and salad rolls'.

Once you have determined the 'measures' though it is critical that you exercise the discipline of tracking and monitoring your results by recording them in the documented form. Just seeing that you have stayed accountable to your plans through your monitoring of measurement will provide enormous encouragement, esteem, and motivation to continue to do the right thing. Measurement is at the heart of all good performance; all great performers in any arena seek to better their best, that is how we improve, but it requires 'measurement'.

The Secrets of Tricking Your Subconscious

Your subconscious mind runs the show. It is so powerful that it will always win out against the conscious mind in a contest of will; which is to say that your 'beliefs' will dictate the level of your commitment to a goal. If you do not 'believe' you can achieve a given goal then no amount of 'hard trying' will get you there. Conversely, if you have belief on your side then extraordinary things are possible; the full force of your whole being and all the universal forces are on your side.

It has been proven without any doubt that the only means of generating belief is through repetition of 'auto suggestion', which is basically 'self-talk'; the great religions know this, it is how prayer works. We all talk to ourselves; maybe not out loud in open debate but certainly, there is an internal dialogue going on inside our head (and for many of us the talk is not positive).

What we say to ourselves regularly, with feeling becomes our beliefs – this is critical because our beliefs flow into our thoughts, our thoughts determine our feelings, our feeling define our actions and our actions dictate our outcomes. If we can engineer beliefs and thoughts, which empower us to feel the way we need to for achieving, desired results; this is the natural course for those in the business who successfully achieve their goals.

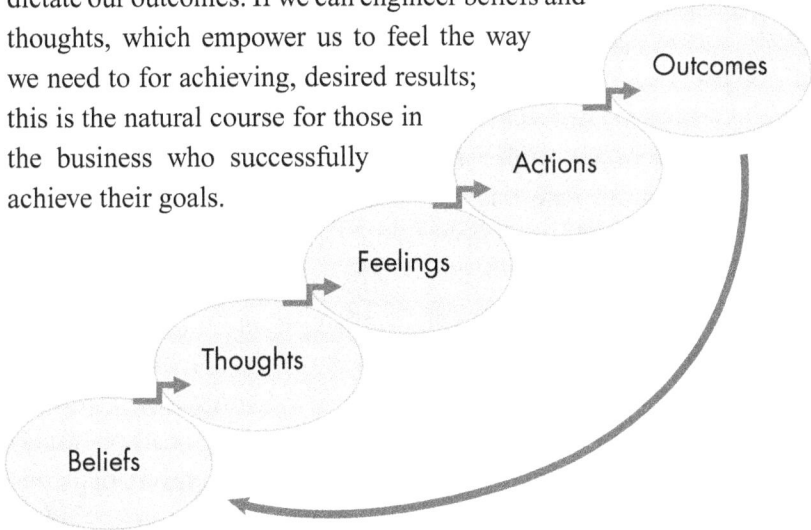

Outcomes

Actions

Feelings

Thoughts

Beliefs

When considering the power of belief it is smart to use this power when setting, pursuing, and achieving our goals. But how? The answer to this question lies in 'Affirmations' and 'Visualization'. Affirmations are positive statements framed in present tense that depict your desired outcome as if already achieved, with attached feelings of having achieved the desired result. For example, 'I run six kilometres, four times per week, feel great, run half marathon and weigh 73 kilograms'.

You should have an affirmation for each of your goals that help power you with belief and state it aloud after you wake and before you go to sleep, (when you are relaxed, and your subconscious is within reach).

Visualization is something commonly referred to with regard to sports psychology and elite sport but like affirmations, it is also the domain of every successful person. You need to see the pictures of your having achieved your goals with as much vivid detail as possible and 'feel' the associated feelings of having attained the outcome you want. It is important to get the 'feeling' of having achieved when doing your affirmations and visualization to generate the belief that will empower you to effective action.

Several years ago I had a client that shared with our Mastermind group, an experience he had with visualization and why he will even now, prefer to be late for a meeting, if it means he can have a few minutes to himself visualizing the desired outcome. This client was a principal at a franchised real estate office in the suburbs of Perth. Several years before that, he was attending a week-long conference at Darling Harbour in Sydney and was finished by lunchtime on the Friday. His flight was scheduled for 6 pm and he was in no hurry to sit at the airport. Instead, he took a walk around Darling Harbour, to look at the boats on display at the boat show that had opened that day and was to run through that weekend.

He saw a boat that he particularly liked. This boat was very large and very expensive, but he was curious and had the time…. He was very impressed with the boat and got into some light banter with the sales consultant, who (after my client had shared with him that he could never afford this boat) gave my client the brochure, which included a very large picture of the vessel on the front cover.

Upon his return to Perth, this client cut the picture of this boat from the front of the brochure (which was more the size of a prospectus, than a brochure) and pasted it on his office wall, just above his computer screen. He looked at this picture on and off (consciously and subconsciously) for nearly 12 months, and then something really interesting happened: he started to perform at a completely new level. In another six months, he was able to call that vessel his own.

The two issues that embedded this discussion in my mind, were (1) it was when he started to link his sales closes to parts of his boat that his sales skyrocketed -referring to a big sale he made as "my fly bridge"; and (2) that it cost nearly $2,000 to fill the fuel tanks - which gives you some idea, as to the size of this boat.

It is important to understand that we will naturally 'visualize' and 'affirm' without effort but what we see and hear 'without effort' is unlikely to help us towards our goals. In 'Think And Grow Rich', Napoleon Hill likens our mind to a garden where your planting of positive seeds of possibility with pictures and words of your choosing you will develop powerful positive belief to aid your goal pursuit, however if left untended, the subconscious will be overrun with the weeds of negative possibility to engulf you with worry, doubt and fear.

Your subconscious mind will fulfill whatever it focuses on and believes, so ensure you have this powerful facility work for you and not against you; use affirmations and visualization to help achieve your goals. Remember that your goals provide the greatest means for clarity and motivation for action so dedicate the time and energy to defining them, documenting them, planting and nurturing the subconscious seed to your success and monitoring your progress.

You CAN achieve great things when you diligently work on your goals. It is particularly important that the business Driver has a firm grasp of setting and achieving goals for himself and his team members. Setting the goals is only the first step; the consistent and diligent pursuit of goals by the Driver and his encouragement of others to confidently pursue theirs are at the heart of the business vehicle achieving its objectives.

SUMMARY POINTS

☑ On the highway of life when there is an accident, you can either sob 'poor me', run away in denial or assess the situation, reset and continue. The third option is the entrepreneurial response

☑ Goal setting is the central factor in motivation and success

☑ Goals need to be S.M.A.R.T – Specific, Measurable, Attainable, Relevant, and Time bound.

☑ Align your personal goals with your business goals

☑ Goals need to be measurable and monitored

☑ Your subconscious runs the show; you need to reach it with visualization and affirmations and generate real belief in your goals

CHAPTER 5
The Controls – Have Profit Drivers Work For You

"*Make every thought, every fact, that comes into your mind pay you a profit. Make it work and produce for you. Think of things not as they are but as they might be. Don't merely dream - but create!*"

Robert Collier

CHAPTER 5

THE CONTROLS – HAVE PROFIT DRIVERS WORK FOR YOU

To double your net earnings in a 6-10 month interval, without the turbulence of business interruption, you will need to know exactly where you are and where you need to be, as well as have measurable milestones along this path that will allow you to prove you are on-track to achieving these objectives. This is not a "business makeover" solution, but a method for business-owners to get their business out of the slow lane and into the express lane, buy small, planned, incremental changes and the method of measuring these.

For most employees, the word CHANGE will generate fear and in some cases, resentment. I understand this, as in most cases, this bad feeling stems from their interaction with the management consultant who facilitated the change, and I am a management consult who has delivered many a redundancy notice as part of my mandate with struggling businesses.

When business owners want to get serious about improving their business, they are almost always referring to an increase in their net profits. Only when these business owners begin to appreciate the number of variables that contribute to that change in their net earnings, will they be able to focus on a continuous improvement journey that will yield far more benefits than just additional earnings. Once a business is automated, the business owner is free from any operational role and can focus on spending less than a day a week managing the business, through monitoring of key indicators and changes.

In order to get a business to that level of efficiency rapidly, you can either get yourself an MBA or equivalent, or you can hire a competent consultant to implement the processes and teach you what he has done. But what if there is another way?

For any business owner to be sufficiently motivated to embark on a full-scale self-development journey, they have to experience how easy and effective managed change can be. This chapter is designed to give you the easiest and most effective change processes, which will deliver an immediate and most profound change in your net earnings. This set of tools is generally the first solution any competent management consultant will implement in your business, because these tools will have the greatest, most immediate, positive impact on your net earnings, than just about any other process. They are called profit drivers, or profit triggers.

The thing that sets profit drivers apart from any other management consultant tool is that they are immediately evident and a management consultant can justify his on-going engagement by having paid for his services ten-fold or more, in the first month of his engagement.

If you could only take one thing from this book, for your business management arsenal, you should learn and implement the profit drivers. If you implement all profit drivers in a business, you can very easily double your annual earnings, in some cases without much investment. So what are these five profit drivers that consultants don't like to share? They are:

- New Customers
- Average Sale Value
- Frequency

- Fixed Costs

- Variable Costs

To best explain these, I will use some practical examples of Australian clients, where we played with the profit drivers and effected immediate and significant change, to rescue or grow a business substantially. I will provide an explanation of the profit drivers in any "for-profit" business and explain how minor incremental improvements can increase on-going profit in an organisation exponentially, with a multiplier effect when two or more profit drivers are adjusted.

The most significant change for profit drivers is in the sale value of a business, as the profitability increases and the annual sales multiplier takes effect, the sale value is exponentially increased. These profit drivers are the most important tools that any manager should carry with them to apply to nearly every business or division that is under-performing, for an immediate and positive change in the earnings and the value.

Increasing the Number of Customers:

If you were to take more than 95% of businesses available today and you were able to immediately increase the number of customers they have by 25%, what do think would happen to their bottom lines? So, what if there were proven methods and directions for most businesses to focus on, doubling their number of customers? Most professional business buyers know what these techniques are and when they acquire a new business they immediately set about implementing these techniques to build the gross profit and more importantly, the business value. There is no surprise here, but if you were to double the number of customers, you should expect to double your earnings.

This is not strictly the case. Firstly, as sales volumes increase, the company should enjoy greater economies of scale, which ensures that the factors of production are reduced. i.e. As your volume increases, your buy-price from suppliers should be reduced. Then, as the personnel and other resources within the firm are better utilised, delivering a greater than 100% increase in net earnings, your variable costs are reduced across the entire production run and the fixed costs remain unchanged for double the number of customers.

Just getting twice as many customers may not always be the perfect solution. Firstly, the types of customers are also critical to your production and delivery systems, so you need to know what would constitute an A-customer (premium) and a B-customer (regular), as distinct from a C-customer (whom you may be better off without). In some circumstances, as you near your production capacity, you may elect to cull some C-customers, by reviewing their individual pricing or other more creative methods.

For example, you may have a customer who only buys from you at sales and rarely pays the list price for anything you offer. He may still be one of your largest buyers, but his profitability and relevant worth would be substantially less to you. If you measured and ranked customers on net profit per customer per year (this is the true value of CRM packages, as cumbersome as most are) the evidence presents itself very quickly.

This principle does not advocate turning away customers. For instance, you may set about turning C-customers into B-customers by simply serving them with a price increase. Alternatively, you may look at acquiring them with the intention of selling them, bundled in a book of clients. For example, I have a real estate agency client who has a substantial property rent roll in the suburbs of Perth. Every year, he identifies 10% of his clients who may have properties that lie outside (or on the edge of) his working territory. He bundles these and makes an approach to other agents in those areas and offers to swap properties in these postcodes, for properties they may have in his postcode. These are valued in the formal practice method as used by the business broking industry ($2 for every gross annual dollar) and the exchange is effected by a joint letter to both the property owner and the tenant(s). The net result for this agency is that over the past 8 years, the managed properties have become far more dense (with less travel time for property managers) and his average value has increased. Economies of scale are immediate and his potential C-clients have become B-clients, by geographical adjustment. He has several properties outside of his preferred postcodes, but these are generally for a strategic reason (most of these are owned by one property group and he wants to manage their entire portfolio).

Secondly, until you calculate the lifetime value of your average customer and compare it to each individual customer, you may not be aware of the true value of each and the value of retaining existing customers in comparison to replacing these with new customers. It is generally about 5-7 times more costly to find a new customer than it is to retain an existing one according to most service business trading models.

However, with the advent of the Internet, entirely new channels are opening up for our businesses and those that embrace this technology can very quickly build a separate channel of interested prospects, which can (with the right feed of regular information) reduce their deliberation cycle by up to 80%. These buyers and prospects are generally not restricted by geographic boundaries and will pounce on information that may help them to qualify the items or services they want to eventually buy.

We have all seen the banner adverts on Google and other websites for, "The 6 key things to avoid when selecting…" and "The top five reasons people regret buying…" They blink at us from the side of the pages we read and if we have any interest in the type of service and/or product on offer, we are inclined to click on them to increase our knowledge in these areas. Once there, we are not subjected to "hard-sell" tactics or asked for our credit cards, but rather we are provided with interesting and (usually) obligation-free information and invited to subscribe to a feed of news or emails that will increase our knowledge in this area. And so, their "learning how to buy" journey begins – with you.

When interviewing a retailer to assess his business, a consultant colleague asked a common question: "How many customers do you have?" The retailer responded immediately with, "In the last week, around 1,800". The consultant (not the most tactful person) shot back, "No you don't", he said",you had 1,800 sales, but how many of those were regulars, how many were first-time buyers, how many were casual buyers and how many were loyal buyers?" The realisation sank in immediately. Without the numbers, how could this retailer improve his number of customers? Worse still, if he couldn't identify them, how could he make customised offers to each of them to increase their loyalty and help them spend more in his store?

This was cured within a week. We placed a static display (an iPad under perspex) as a prize near the sale registers. This had a small sign, "Win an iPAD – complete the coupon for your store discount card". Within a week we had many of the buyers completing the cards and placing these in the entry box. The assistants were handing the shoppers a card with their receipt and inviting them to complete this and drop it into the entry barrel below.

In less than a month, the store owner had a statistically-valid profile of his customer demographic, as well as sufficient home addresses and email addresses to start a direct-mail catalogue with specific offers for these loyalty card holders. The catalogue later went city-wide, with a special price below the sale price, for loyalty club members. The database kept growing.

For most businesses, increasing the number of customers is a function of increasing the number of 'leads' or interested parties, and increasing the 'conversion rate' or the proportion of buyers as a result of the leads. There are many, many ways to increase lead generation and in our Formula 1 program we examine nearly eighty five areas of potential lead generation; the only limitations are imagination, belief and commitment. Similarly, with increasing conversion rates there are many ways to improve this metric; we address almost a hundred potential means of increasing conversion; the key comes down to understanding the customer and providing undeniable value.

Increasing the Average Sale Value:

Increasing the average sale value is all about adding increased value for the customer. When our pet store owner sells a Cockatoo, the customer has a need (whether he knows it or not) for a cage, birdseed and a whole bunch of other Cockatoo paraphernalia. Why not assemble a 'Cocky Pack' which includes all the things that the Cocky owner will need for his new feathered friend?

There are opportunities in every business, from professional services to technology products and everything in between, to provide additional services or products which are related to and will augment the initial purchase. It is not only your obligation to do this from the perspective of increasing your earnings but also in the name of optimising the experience of your customer. You are making life better for them by providing more.

This may, at first, appear to be another obvious profit driver, but the ingenuity of this is in the detail. We have all been subjected to ASV increases at the drive through window of fast food outlets, as they continually invite us to upsize or ask if we would like some fries with that? But what about a service industry?

Some time ago, I took our dog for a clip at a dog grooming service. The requirement was to be there to collect the dog at 50 mins after the hour, so that nobody was kept waiting. It took an hour to clip the dog, but in that last 10 minutes I was engaged in conversation with the groomer. The conversation was clearly scripted, but I still bought it.

Her: What brush do you use on your dog?

Me: I don't know, a dog brush…?

Her: It looks like you are using something that is not getting deep enough to comb out the undercoat properly.

Me: Umm…Maybe…

Her: You need a decent brush to get to the undercoat, instead of one of those Kmart ones. We have the proper brushes for your dog, would you like to see one?

Me: Well…OK

Her: (Still working on the dog, not trying to get a brush for me to look at). We have these available for you in our doggy pamper pack. The brushes on their own cost $14.95 but you can get this in the pamper pack for just $19.95. The pamper pack has shampoo and other stuff you will need and you'd be getting all of that for practically nothing. Shall I get you one of these on the way out?

Me: Um…OK

This might not sound like a significant sale, but what has happened here? This person was able to increase the average sale value by $19.95, with an estimated margin of around $14, from a sale of $60. That is a 33% increase in the sale and (once you factor in the wages) even higher on the margin. Her overheads didn't change, the extra time she spent was less than 2 minutes and she didn't have to stop what she was doing to complete the transaction.

This would not have been a once-off accident. This is the result of a carefully prepared script, with a regular review program to ensure the script is followed. I do not doubt that this groomer and all the other staff there felt very awkward and self-conscious about this script when they were first given it – just like we do for the first few dozen times we listen to it at the fast-food drive-through window. Eventually, everybody gets over it and the grooming place is well on their way to increasing their gross profit by up to 30% on a script and a $6 plastic gift pack (which doesn't look different from the Kmart ones…). If that grooming place was to vary their offers every 3-4 months, they would be able to maintain the average sale value and still be perceived as less expensive than their competitors.

There is the legend of a pet store owner who noticed that afternoon shoppers rarely bought more than two items. He studied their behaviours and noticed one important thing, they didn't buy any more because their hands were full. Being early afternoon, most shoppers were time poor and did not get a trolley when they came in. He crafted a script and had his staff rehearse the timing and delivery of this. The instruction was to push an empty trolley past these people as soon as they had picked up a second item. They were to stop alongside the shopper and say, "Here, let me put these in a trolley for you", while they took one of the items from the shopper and placed it in the trolley.

This was not confrontational and was received with gratitude in most cases. You can guess what happened to the average sale value. The average number of items per transaction shot up, as did the length of time each shopper spent in the store, in what was previously deemed "rush-hour". By studying habits and numbers, the store owner was able to increase these numbers by designing, practicing and then perfecting a process to help people shop more easily in his store. He was able to improve his numbers, only because he knew them.

Frequency of Sale:

When we are asked by business owners how many customers they have, they generally talk of sales (as discussed previously). If you know how many transactions you have, then the number of customers is going to be less, based on the frequency of which they buy. If you get to know how many customers you have, you can then divide this by the transactions and you have your average frequency of sale. This is important, because it becomes a metric to measure your improvement.

There are some (very few) businesses that only provide a service once, while other businesses have many transactions, but may have no details of their customers. There are very compelling reasons to have this information, including the way that business brokers will value your business. One of the most effective methods of gathering data on your customers (particularly for retail) is to tempt them with an apple, as we discussed earlier in the "win an iPad" promotion. The most effective way to do this is to hand them cards (or a second printed receipt) with their change, so that they recognise it is important for them to be "invited by purchase" and is not for just anyone who walks in and fills out a form.

Once you have your frequency of sale calculated, you can understand the purchasing cycle or service delivery cycle of your client. This becomes critical to understanding where the bottlenecks in your business model may be, as you plan ways to encourage these customers to shorten their intervals between visits.

For example, if you have 1,000 customers who purchase $100 in services from you every 8 weeks (on average), you will be able to increase your sales by 33% if you are able to reduce their buying cycle to 6 weeks. Imagine an increase in sales of 33% and you haven't had to find one more customer! If your overheads remained the same (particularly for a service business, such as a hairdresser) your gross earnings would be more than the 33% increase.

So what would a 50% increase in gross earnings be worth to you? Would you be prepared to reward these customers for reducing their buying cycle to 6 weeks by offering an additional (small) service as complementary, if they book and come by before a certain date? In most cases, the service you select may not take more time for your bookings, but could be performed concurrently by the operator during the same service interval. In summary, all you have done is provide some extra time, to increase the frequency of the customer's visit, because you have been able to contact the customer directly and send a personal invitation to treat them for their loyalty. Let's look at a hair salon.

If a hair salon has 600 customers each calling in every 8 weeks, spending $100 on average, the value for this salon (without any marketing) would be 6.5 visits per year, by 600 clients by $100. This equates to a total revenue of $390,000. Given that most places operate on 1/3 Fixed Costs and 1/3 Variable Costs (in this case wages) then this would provide approximately $130,000 for gross profit. If I was to offer all 600 clients a free extra service (valued at $25 but costs me $6 in labour) and I offered this for week 5 of their 8-week cycle, I may have a 25% uptake on this.

If I did have this 25% uptake (offer is valid for only one week – specific to that client) and the cycle was now 6 weeks instead of 8 weeks. Some things happen.

450 clients x $100 x 6.5 visits   = $292,500

150 clients x $100 x 8.6 visits   = $129,000

Less the 150 services @ $6 x 8.6   = $7,740

Total earnings on this model is now $421,492

This is an additional $31,492, which is all gross profit dollars! This represents an increase in your earnings of 19.6% for just offering one extra service at their visit. In most cases, the extra service would not cost you anything, if it is just utilising us-billed salon time and if you are offering a special service, wouldn't you have your suppliers provide samples of it on the basis that you are going to offer it free to clients to try? If you were able to implement such a simple idea into your business (and we have done this in all types of businesses, from auto service to chiropractic) imagine what a 25% uptake would mean to your net earnings?

Expenses – Fixed and Variable:

When we initially meet with most small business owners, in most cases the only source of business advice they have received, has been from their accountants. With all due respect to the accounting profession, this advice (in more than 75% of cases in our experience) has been focussed on costs. Although costs can be the most powerful and immediate of the profit drivers, it can also be the most devastating if you get it wrong.

Fixed costs are the most prominent area of focus by accountants. Having provided management consulting services for nearly 25 years, there have been many requests for me to bill my services on the agreed outcomes. This can be frustrating for me (as a professional) and equally dangerous for the client. I usually take a few minutes to explain to them why I will not do this. Here is the core reason not to incentivise a consultant this way.

If I was to agree to, say a $100,000 payment if I was to achieve a $500,000 pa positive net effect on your company gross profit, in whatever time I was able to achieve it, I could get very lazy. I could restructure your company by firing half of the staff and putting fear into the remaining personnel, so that they will carry the process for several months. Although this would not be sustainable, I could prove a net earnings projection that meets my target and then claim my fee on the way out.

Of course, your company would suffer morale and fatigue issues, as well as service standards (if I slashed the key staff who had all the "know-how" and customer loyalty) but couldn't I claim (if you sought to recover any fees from me months later) that it was working fine when I left and you messed it up later?

I recently worked with a small firm which rents vending machines to hotels, clubs and other public venues. They were losing money and could not understand why. When we examined the business model, it was wages. We shifted some of the tasks to others and we outsourced the heavy lifting to contractors so were able to slash the wages bill by 33% with an instant positive cash effect. The difference was that we trialled the planned system before exiting the less productive personnel. We kept the technical experience and we outsourced the heavy stuff, which they felt they needed several people to do, but was performed less than 2 days per month. This company is currently looking for cheaper premises (they realised they do not need a prominent shopfront) and are moving sales and casual hire business to the Internet.

Variable costs are generally the most rewarding for consultants. We can generally help business owners to "discover" hidden value in their variable costs, by asking for it. We have (on more than one occasion) simply drafted a standard letter to all suppliers explaining how we have felt the pinch in the recent months and in order to maintain our long-term relationship, we need to ask for a 10% discount on the current buy price. In some cases, we ask for the higher volume discount on the existing sales schedule, for a fixed period (say 12 months).

We make these letters as specific and as personal as possible, so that suppliers understand that (1) We have studied this carefully, (2) This is the amount we need to make the program work, and (3) We would have no choice than to start searching elsewhere to ensure the survival of our company and to ensure we maintain the standard of service or sales to our customers. In the majority of cases, this single request shaves 10% off the buy price of most goods and services, including from multi-national suppliers! People understand pain and are prepared to share it, if the reward is loyalty.

A regular examination of variable costs will identify where there are opportunities to reduce costs for no reduction in effectiveness. For example, phone plans and providers can be rationalised, particularly with the constantly evolving landscape of phone services. However, it all starts with looking at variable costs and identifying the opportunities for improvement.

Summarising Profit Drivers

To summarise, profit drivers are the most significant metrics that will deliver the most immediate outcomes for your business, in most circumstances. This alone is the most compelling reason that all business owners have to get to know their numbers. Every performance athlete knows that you cannot improve what you can't measure and in most cases all of the measurable metrics are very visible to the business owner.

The metrics that are less visible (in most cases) are required to become visible, so you will need to engineer ways of understanding what your profit drivers are within your business, what the measurables are and then set your "personal best" performance level for your team to exceed and push out over time. Performance athletes do not become the best because they are faster than others. They become best because they incrementally improve their performances through measurement and goal-setting. There should be no difference for your business.

To become the best in your industry, you need to implement this process into your best practice routines. Changes should not be radical as this can impact on your staff just as much as clients. Look for small incremental changes and valid points of measure, to make sure you are doing what you are being paid for – building the business.

One of the most underrated benefits that will emerge from this performance measurement of profit drivers, is the effect it will have on prospective buyers. Your business performance is now measurable and therefore, improvable. Although month-on-month and year-on-year the measurables may not indicate consistent improvement, they will show the trend that strategic planning can be focused upon.

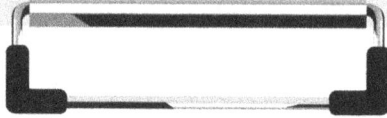

SUMMARY POINTS

☑ You need to have relevant metrics to measure, if you want to improve.

☑ The most effective metrics to manipulate are profit drivers. These have an immediate and direct affect on the net earnings of the business.

☑ The three positive drivers are (1) Increased number of customers, (2) Increased average-sale-value, and (3) Increased frequency of sales.

☑ The two negative drivers are (1) Reduce variable costs, and (2) Reduce fixed costs.

☑ Successful business owners know their profit drivers and study and change these on a regular basis.

CHAPTER 6
Vehicle Information (Managing the Available Data)

"If you can't measure it, you can't manage it."

Peter Drucker

CHAPTER 6
VEHICLE INFORMATION
(MANAGING THE AVAILABLE DATA)

Commit to Incremental Improvement?

It may not surprise many that the top coaches of any sports endeavour are nearly always able to pick champions before they are champions. The question for most observers is, "Are they able to pick them or do they make them?"

The secret for most coaches is very similar. For example, a track and field coach who may be seeking to recruit his next champion in a particular event; as track and field events are generally not team sports, the coach is recruiting individuals.

His first step is to muster the candidates he would like to select from. He would run a try-out event to narrow the field by eliminating those who are not really in contention. He may then look for fitness, self-care, technique and recovery times. His next objective would be to take the remaining candidates and form a training squad for a period of time. His objective is to set and measure each candidate and their performance over the period. What is less well known is that top coaches do not necessarily pick the fastest or the best at that time. They would generally select the candidate that demonstrates the most consistent incremental improvement (CII) during that training squad period.

The demonstration of consistent incremental improvement by any candidate is a much better indication of a potential champion. If the fastest candidate does not demonstrate improvement, they may have peaked or perhaps reached their mental capacity and will not be able to improve over time. With a consistent improvement model, the CII candidate will eventually become faster than the fastest candidate and could go on to become the World Champion.

This is how we should select and later promote our key personnel, in particular, our sales personnel. In the athletic model, the candidates who consistently improve, recognise that they compete against themselves. In interviews after races you can hear the chatter of the winning athletes, which will generally focus on their personal best (PBs) and not the other competitors. They know they have to beat themselves to get to that race and then beat their best times to finish first.

In operating a highly competitive business, you mostly compete against yourself. The most outstanding companies don't get too focussed on the competitors, they focus on their own performance and improve that. By consistent improvements and changes they make to their business or market models, they will eventually become the best.

One of the business school traps in this area is benchmarking. Whilst it is important to know how you currently sit within your competitive environment, you should not set a goal to be better than the industry's top performer (as measured now) within five years, because it is likely that any competitor that is not achieving that level of activity would not be in business by then. This would like striving for mediocrity.

Data Management by Exception

In any motor racing team the manager and the driver do not need to know temperature gauge readouts during a race. The exception to this rule is if the readout is showing a performance level outside the acceptable parameters. In business, we call this exception reporting.

Several years ago, in a prominent annual 1,000km motor race in Bathurst, Australia, one of the competitors (and then race leader) had the misfortune of having a plastic bag (discarded by one of the thousands of spectators) sweep into his front grill, thereby blocking off his oil cooler and radiator air intake. This immediately caused the operating temperature to increase, as less air was able to pass through the oil cooler and the radiator.

Under exception reporting, it would then become critical for the pit crew to monitor this condition and for the crew manager to make a decision to (a) Direct the driver to make a pit stop, (b) Direct the driver to drive more conservatively, by not slipstreaming, etc., or (3) Continue to drive his race and hope the engine did not destroy itself before the finish line. Without this condition, there would have been no requirement for the driver or the crew to monitor this indicator as closely as they did, but when it was outside the acceptable operating range, it was immediately important.

If you ever stepped into the cockpit of a large airliner, the first thing that would impress you would be the number of gauges. On my first introduction to the cockpit, I could not understand how any pilot could possibly monitor all of those gauges during flight, and still look out of the aircraft. Exception reporting is the key.

Firstly, in straight and level flight, under normal conditions, most analogue instruments have a default position of vertical up. This enables the pilot to scan the instruments on a regular basis and only lock in on any indicator that is not pointing directly up.

In more modern aircraft, the instrument panel has indicators, as well as led indicators, which will glow orange or red in the event that they are operating marginally or outside of the standard operating range.

In business, we may have up to 100 daily or weekly indicators that demonstrate the health of the business. However, as managers, we must balance our time between the planning, organisation, leadership and control of all our resources.

Control (monitoring and adjusting resources) cannot take up the majority of our time, so we prepare an aggregation of key performance indicators for a daily and/or weekly summary, which will enable us to 'scan the instruments' and determine the health of the business on a regular basis. This way we are only responding to exceptions, or a priority basis. When something is not normal, we need to seek more information to qualify, clarify or eliminate it as a problem.

The summary of KPIs (your aggregated list of indicators) is generally termed your scorecard. There are many useful KPI scorecard programs available for business managers who would like to automate this monitoring and control function, so they can spend more time on planning, organisation and leadership of the organisations resources.

When you prepare your business for sale (covered in later chapters) having a KPI scorecard program implemented, will directly and positively affect your selling price. This is one of the key instruments to free the principal from working within his business on a full-time basis.

It is not hard to remotely receive and interpret meaningful data on the business on a daily or weekly basis, and plan the required corrective action to ensure growth is continuous. The most critical aspect of this function is that the business principal does not need to be present to monitor the business and can request more meaningful data when any one KPI is operating outside the acceptable limitation.

How Do We Measure Business Performance?

Firstly, we have stated in previous chapters that if you can't measure something, you can't improve it. This also means that you will not be able to tell immediately if performance is slipping or improving, despite the performance of the cash position.

If you have a 40% off sale, cash will be abundant but inventory will be depleting rapidly. If you measure banking as your only metric, you may feel you are doing quite well. However, there is a real cost of replacement that could soak up far more than you expected. So, what are the important numbers here? Let's firstly look at building your most relevant indicators, as either critical success factors (CSFs) or key performance indicators (KPIs).

The examples of key performance indicators and critical success factors are used intermittently in this chapter, as it is deemed more relevant to provide a practical message, rather than a concise academic definition for the reader. The most prevalent difference for these is that CSFs will measure a single metric, whereas KPIs will measure one metric in direct relation to another, providing a ratio rather than a unit. Both can be plotted and in some cases, the complexity of the latter may not provide a greater proportional benefit than the former.

Key performance indicators are essentially metrics we use to measure all aspects of a business, to ensure wellness. Think of that pilot scanning his instruments – he needs to be able to tell at a glance if everything is fine. He needs a red light (visual) and buzz (audio) alerts to any critical exceptions to his "normal". If you operate a business and you don't wish to sit in there controlling every minute detail, then you will need to receive and analyse the firm's performance data at a glance, on a regular basis.

People who can't let go of their business can be likened to the engineer on the plane, who doesn't want to look at the instruments, but wants to go and have a look at the hydraulics or the electrical harness, etc., to satisfy himself all is OK. This can be far more accurate, but can cost him all of his available time. In any emergency, the pilot does not have the luxury of time.

Before we build a dashboard or scorecard (the aggregated summary of all metrics we intend to measure) we need to review the structure we want and to ensure we have asked the right questions of this process, in order to build the most effective KPI reporting system. The types of questions we should be asking ourselves are:

- Which metrics will show how well you are tracking towards your vision and strategy?

- How many metrics should you measure? (The temptation is to overdo it.)

- How often should you measure? (Monthly, quarterly, annually?)

- Which group, department or individual is accountable for the metric?

- How complex should the metric be? Can it be easily understood by everyone?

- What should you use as your industry comparison or benchmark?

- How do you ensure the metrics will reflect the agreed strategies for the organisation?

- How can the metrics be manipulated and how will you prevent this?

- What negative, detrimental incentives can be triggered by this and how will you ensure these negative incentives are not created?

Once you have established meaningful metrics for measuring organisational or employee performance, you now have to make sure that the supporting elements of employee performance and reward are aligned as well. It is important to tie reward to achievement and the more closely you achieve this, the more incentive you build into your performance measurement system. For example, you might have a KPI that measures how many new customers are attracted to the business each week. Depending on the situation, a well-aligned performance system may reward employees based on the number of new customers they personally help to attract, rather than sharing a reward based on overall numbers.

The key to establishing and measuring the right business indicators in your dashboard is to always focus on aggregating like and linked metrics. For an example, I will use a sales organisation. Many years ago, in my early 20s, I was employed by and later became a partner in a small training company in Adelaide. We trained non-sales managers in sales, so that they understood how to negotiate. We also showed them how trained negotiators would use particular techniques on them in their working environment. This could result in a big shift (either way) on concessions, in any sales or negotiations. In feedback sessions, most of these people conceded that they used these techniques to negotiate a better employment deal – either a pay-rise or a promotion.

The trainee delegates were middle managers and branch managers from non-sales related fields, such as banking. We gave them a product to sell, so they all had a level playing field to use their techniques. The product we chose was gift voucher booklets, offered on behalf of registered charities. We gave them a 15 minute briefing on the charity and a 15 min brief on the product, including a structured sales script to follow and a "territory" of 100 doors to knock on (any suburban main road of their choice).

We measured the number of doors they knocked on, the number of attempts they made to present their script, the number of times they completed their script and the number of sales they made (sometimes more than one per house). Finally, we counted the cash per hour to calculate their hourly value as an employee of that charity. Interesting information started to emerge.

Firstly, people got really embarrassed doing door-knocking and generally picked a street on the other side of town from where they lived or worked. We pointed out that sales were higher in lower socio-economic suburbs, but these trainees generally picked the more affluent suburbs.

Then, we started to examine the KPIs and identified several more things.

Those who followed the script had more consistent sales.

Some trainees had very poor numbers but good sales (We confronted them about buying booklets for themselves – this distorts the stats).

When we got the poor sellers back onto the scripts, they all improved.

We could tell where they were falling down, just by the change in ratios, we could then tweak their script and sales flowed.

Without exception, they all hated it but they all agreed it was beneficial. We proved KPIs will drive sales.

We could look at the stats and identify within seconds where the person was deviating from the plan, why they were not performing, how to increase their effectiveness and if they were cheating, all without going out into the streets with them.

One important issue for building KPIs is the number of KPIs per person. It is generally considered that a workable number of KPIs on any single dashboard for any employee or manager is six. For maximum effect, these can be plotted on an XY chart with other personnel, as well as past year performances in a different colour for comparison.

Let us now use the description of KPIs to define the areas of measure for small business. The most important primary KPI measures for most businesses under the $10m turnover, are sales, customers, staff, process and financial KPIs, followed by secondary KPIs, such as quality control and industry benchmarking.

Sales (Customer) Measures

If you have a sales-focused company, it is always best to start with sales and work backwards through the process (production/service delivery, etc.) before then looking at marketing. Most organisations refer to this as a sales funnel.

If you have a business that sells services, then you need to measure your performance in service delivery AND in the gaining and retention of customers. We typically break the sales funnel into sections such as:

Lead generation. Every growing business needs to measure how many new prospects are being brought into the business system. If there are insufficient new prospects, the sales department starts to slow (that goes for businesses which do not have a sales department – where everybody becomes the sales department). If you measure the number of new prospects captured into the customer relationship management (CRM) system, you can stay well ahead of the decline curve, by adjusting your promotion budget (advertising, networking, etc.) well ahead of the sales activity.

Database membership. In this day of online marketing and internet buying, we need to get sophisticated about the way we treat every inquiry to our business or our website. Our first instinct is to sell these visitors something, but our core objective should be to deliver them some informative data that confirms your value to them and will result in their completing a registration form to receive more information on the products or services. We need to remember that (particularly online) visitors are not necessarily looking to buy immediately, but may be looking for information on "how to buy" the product or service they require.

By capturing the contact, you can create an informative database of information seekers to which you can provide regular updates, to ensure they can receive the complete information from you, making your firm the primary source of information pertaining to their need. You will effectively become the trusted party. This makes your sales teams' job far easier, as they ring this list to make appointments to present their product or service.

Conversion to appointments. This metric is also referred to as lead conversion. In this age of shares and electronic diaries, this is one of the easiest KPIs to measure. Ensuring activity is up and records are kept is easy. All you need to insist on is that all call activity is recorded in the CRM and this will immediately qualify the call quality and/or the sales capabilities. If there are 12 calls per week for three sales as an average for the sales team, you can quickly see if a rep is averaging

12-15 calls and getting one sale. This person either needs sales training, better prospecting skills or is working on other things and inventing activity to make their efforts look better. You now know where you need to focus your efforts.

Completed presentations. Through the CRM data, you can determine how many of the sales calls were effective. It could be that the principal was not able to see the rep on that day and the appointment has been reset for another day. However, if this rep is consistently calling and not completing a presentation, they are effectively burning territory for you. The solution may be sales training or replacement, but you will be able to determine this immediately if you have access to the information on a weekly basis and you average this against the group and/or the past. This metric will measure itself and you can set your CRM system to deliver you an exception report against individuals compared and contrasted with the group average.

Sales (units) and revenues. This is the single most measured metric in most companies. However, to have the most appropriate meaning, the sales totals need to be broken down. The most meaningful measure is gross profit, which will measure unit sales by sale price, less cost. This will adjust the sales volume to compensate for price. If a sales rep is discounting the product by 20% (and your GP margin is 30%) they would have to sell three times the volume of other sales personnel, to maintain the expected gross profit. It could be that this rep is making the same amount of gross profit per month, but burning through three times the prospects to achieve this. This activity would invoke corrective action for a business manager.

Repeats and referrals. This measure is sometimes referred to as customer retention and moves away from the internal activity and towards the customer experience. In most cases, if the purchasing experience was satisfying to the buyer, their next need should be directed to your firm. This cannot be taken for granted (they may receive in the mail a 50% off catalogue from your competitor, on the day they are looking to buy) but in most cases, the measure of repeats and referrals is an excellent indicator of the level of customer satisfaction. This can be measured with loyalty programs, surveys and through mining your CRM to identify the ratio of R & R with each rep and with the online system.

General Customer Measures

This set of measures is oriented to customer success and should be more aligned to the corporate goals, rather than the individual performance goals. These would be used to measure the sales department as well as the organisational health as a rule, but if there appears to be anomalies, the reader should then drill down to individual KPIs within the sales and/or marketing departments to gauge a clearer position. Some of the more frequently-used customer measures include:

Cost per customer. This can be a single metric of the total marketing expense averaged over the number of new customers within the measured interval, or it can be an aggregate of several factors, including effort and achievements by sales personnel, retention efforts and expense as well as the value of each customer (gross profit) against the marginal extra expense of recruiting him.

Cost/Value per order. This metric becomes a direct measure of how sales personnel offer additional products or services, with cross-selling and up-selling opportunities. When a customer is buying, having the customer add services to their principal purchase will not increase the sales cost by anything other than the marginal cost of the goods or services. Individuals should be recognised and rewarded for increasing the average sale value of every transaction. This recognition will embed the habit to become standard procedure for each team member, if managed correctly.

Sales frequency. In earlier chapters we discussed ways of increasing the frequency of which customers buy from the business. This measure records and displays this to gauge how well the individual client account rep is managing this frequency and if the marketing program is helping or hindering.

Customer retention. Although this metric appears at first glance to be a corporate measure, it is critical to measure customers against their allocated sales personnel, with the aggregate of all sales personnel (and customers) against the corporate mission. This would place the individual performance on the individual sales reps dashboard, and the aggregate on the sales manager and CEO's dashboard as an overall measure of the sales departments' health.

These sales KPIs should allow firms to measure individuals, teams, regions, etc. against their own benchmarks, as well as against their competitors, where such data is compiled.

In most cases, managers confuse team KPIs with sales KPIs. When this happens, you miss the most important internal metric in any organisation, how well the team performs as a collective and cohesive entity, rather than as a group of individuals who see their competition as each other.

Process Measures

Product mix performance. For any organisation to remain relevant, the senior management must periodically review and determine the contribution, relevance and complementary relationship of each individual product or revenue source, to all others. When one line consistently underperforms, the reasons may be many and varied. These should be identified and the product subject to a periodic review to determine if it should remain in the portfolio or sold.

It could be that one product is facing greater competition that others and may require a differentiation strategy or an aggressive pricing position for a period. It could be that buyers no longer need or want that product and are buying something else from your own or others range.

Advertising effectiveness. In 1903, one of the most prominent Philadelphia retailers of the day (Mr John Wannamaker) made a famous statement: "I know that half of my advertising budget is wasted – I just can't tell which half!" There have been many developments in advertising spend tracking, but for all I have seen, there has only been one program that will track every medium (print, TV, billboard, etc.), across every event (day, time, intensity, etc.) for every product or service line in an organisation.

At the time of this book going to press, that product had just completed trials with one of the largest advertising agency networks across Australia and was about to be made available to advertising and marketing managers and media planners/buyers. At the risk of sounding like a sales message, I urge you to investigate this for yourselves. The product is known as Q-metrics and is an Australian innovation.

Inventory management. This metric is generally kept within the accounting department, because of the immediate and severe effect it can have on the cash flow and profitability of a business. A savvy management accountant will calculate the lead-time for individual suppliers and the processing time for product delivery, against the levels of inventory being retained in store. In most cases, an internal inventory holding cost is placed against each item, to ensure the lowest levels of inventory are carried, thereby reducing the amount of cash tied up in inventory and reducing the exposure of the company to shifts in client buying trends.

Shipping. In some cases, it is important for firms to measure the delivery lead-times and the error rates on shipping. Measuring metrics like order-processing times, lead-times from delivery to commissioning, incomplete or wrong goods shipped or damaged goods received, can identify the true cost of mistakes and identify if the same person is making them.

Safety and injury prevention. Firms with industrial plant will generally have a strong occupational health program and will measure performance per department and for the plant, on injury-free days. In some cases, these can be aggregated to the CEO's accountabilities and a group bonus evenly distributed to all members of the team, so everyone assumes responsibility for worker safety and accident prevention.

Financial Measures

Accounting standards will refer to ratios for measuring the liquidity and operational stability of a company, at its present moment. Ratios give users an 'idea' of the ability of a company to meet its short-term liabilities with its short-term assets. Another beneficial use is to compare the quick ratio with the current ratio. If the current ratio is significantly higher, it is a clear indication that the company's current assets are dependent on inventory.

Current Ratio

This ratio is mainly used to give an overview of the company's ability to pay back its short-term liabilities (debt and payables) with its short-term assets (cash, inventory and receivables). The higher the current ratio, the more capable the company is of paying its obligations. A ratio under one suggests that the company would be unable to pay off its obligations if they came due at that point. While this shows the company is not in good financial health, it does not necessarily mean that it will go bankrupt - as there are many ways to access financing - but it does demand attention.

The current ratio can give a sense of the efficiency of a company's operating cycle or its ability to turn its product into cash. Companies that have trouble getting paid on their receivables or have long inventory turnover can run into liquidity problems because they are unable to alleviate their obligations. Because business operations differ in each industry, it is always more useful to compare companies within the same industry.

Quick Ratio

The quick ratio is a more conservative version of the other well-known liquidity metric - the current ratio. Although the two are similar, the quick ratio provides a more rigorous assessment of a company's ability to pay its current liabilities.

The quick ratio does this by eliminating all but the most liquid of current assets from consideration. Inventory is the most notable exclusion, because it is not as rapidly convertible to cash and is often sold on credit. Some analysts include inventory in the ratio though, if it is more liquid than certain receivables.

Other Ratios

There are many other types of ratios in use by management accountants, but these are not generally used as much to assess business value but valuers. These other types have terms like acid test ratio, current liabilities, current assets, working capital ratio, inventory turnover ratio, receivables ratio, the liquidity test and the key ratio.

Industry KPIs – Benchmarking

In many popular industries, aggregated performance data for firms is shared and measured to enable all industry players to compare and contrast their monthly and quarterly performance against their competitors in the local, national and (in some cases) global markets. This is known as benchmarking data. Some industries (such as finance, insurance, banking and real estate) have more sophisticated data sets and in some cases, going back more than 50 years.

If you measure it, you can improve it. The key is sustainable and incremental improvements. If you set your benchmarks to achievable levels, you then set your rewards to celebrate each incremental improvement milestone, as you THEN move the benchmark to the new improved standard. Of critical importance, astute managers link the staff bonus system to a split between individual KPIs (to ensure best performance) and collective KPIs (to engender team cooperation) for maximum impact and effectiveness.

Continuous Improvement

Continuous improvement is often referred to by the Japanese word 'Kaizen' which translates to 'change for the better' and was designed to cover all processes in an organisation. The more popular areas of focus for CI is R & D, design and engineering, production, inventory management, information technology, financial, commercial and customer service processes. Continuous improvement is dependent on strong measurement and management of performance data.

This process should be established and implemented by a strategic planning team or a technical advisory panel, which (regardless of the size of the business) should involve trusted people outside the organisation, for some balance and objectivity. The process of CI involves making continual small incremental improvements to a business process rather than big changes at irregular intervals. This requires close monitoring and control, changes to the usage of manpower, machinery, methods, materials and resources in order to improve the business efficiency.

Continuous improvement starts with management (through vision and objectives) and under their leadership, works down through the organisation. The underlying theme is that everyone is responsible and has a part to play in making improvements. All employees must work together to identify the steps needed to improve working practices. Planning meetings help teams to focus on the greater strategic planning objectives and maintain a focus on customer needs.

Developing efficiency is only one aspect of continuous improvement. The other core tenant is reduction of waste. This involves focusing on any activity or process that does not directly add value. A key question to define waste is to ask, 'Would a customer pay for that process?' There are several core areas of waste for most businesses:

- Transportation and storage - moving materials or products about

- Inventory - keeping too much or the wrong stock and in the wrong location

- Motion - people moving or travelling excessively

- Down times - allowing products or components to wait for processing

- Over production - making too much of any production unit

- Over processing - doing too many stages or processes during manufacture

- Defects - errors or flaws in the product causing rework or needing to be scrapped

Production processes that minimise waste are referred to as "lean production". In these processes, the aim is to use less of everything, for example, space, people, materials or time. With incremental improvement as a process, we design and embed a culture of collecting feedback to set the right priorities to drive the change process. The more feedback you get, the better you will be able to evolve your process. So let's take a look at what your change process needs to include.

- Feedback Records with Deficiency Notations

- Trend Analysis

- Corrective Action Process and Criteria for Action

- Audit Process

Management Review Process

Once you have delivered the right answers to the strategic planning team, they will need to match the change process against the corporate vision, for total congruence. As part of this process, accurate change and feedback records need to be kept and used.

Once processes are documented, the reviewers can scrutinise these for business process inefficiencies. Once they identify some inefficiency, they should have these analysed for statistical significance, so that resources are focused only on those issues that matter. Once these inefficiencies have been addressed with a corrective action, the CI committee should document how and when the corrective or preventive action is to be implemented and what resources need to be allocated to the change in process (if any).

It is essential that all proposed changes be checked to ensure they are consistent with the vision and strategic plan of the company. There should also be an objective review of all processes to ensure the change process is working and some key personnel are nominated to be accountable for the review and reporting to the CI committee.

Finally, the strategic planning team will need to review all findings to ensure the change process is working and the objectives (efficiency, effectiveness, savings, etc.) are achieved. More importantly, does it move the company towards the vision and core objectives?

All of the measures, ratio's and continuous improvement perspectives put forward in this chapter are means to managing more effectively through measurement and monitoring of the data in your business. Just as a race car has many measures which will be key indicators of performance so will your business vehicle. It is critical to establish these measures and continue the discipline of monitoring them to maximise your speed around the business race track.

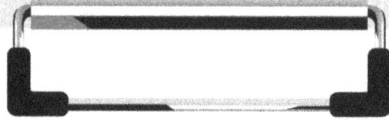

SUMMARY POINTS

☑ To reduce our information overload we need to focus on exception reporting, only looking at what isn't right.

☑ To achieve this, we need a dashboard of metrics that will deliver an aggregated overview of the organisation's performance and health.

☑ The best metrics are key performance indicators and financial ratios.

☑ The business should be measured at regular intervals, to ensure that any changes are delivering the desired outcomes and not detrimentally affecting other areas.

CHAPTER 7
Turbo Boost –
Supercharging your Sales

*"The definition of salesmanship is the gentle
art of letting the customer have it your way."*

Ray Kroc

CHAPTER 7
TURBO BOOST
– SUPERCHARGING YOUR SALES

The New Paradigm in Marketing and Sales

Have you ever wondered why car salesmen and real estate salesmen are very pushy? It's very simple, really. Only the pushy ones survive because being nice makes it too hard to survive with the volume of sales required. You see, buyers only buy a car every 4-6 years on average and have very little buyer experience (knowledge on how to buy a car) and so we are all green about what we can and/or can't say or do. We don't understand our role in the transaction.

It may not be a surprise to learn that all of these salesmen are following a carefully crafted and practiced script, which includes answers to all of your possible objections to their close (the request for an order). The good ones all sound very natural, but it is the same script and in most cases, it has to get them the result they need, in a 10-20 minute interaction, while you are distracted by the shiny new car.

These car salesmen have to establish a rapport with you in less than 2 minutes and from this basis of a business relationship, must pressure you to buy their car, or you will be pressured equally by the next guy and they will get nothing. We hate this experience, but they don't care – they need to get to your decision as quickly as possible, at the highest price possible.

Do you want to have some fun with these guys? Why not prepare a series of questions that they could not have thought of and put them through their paces. These don't have to be technical questions. Ask things such as, "What kind of aura does this car show when it is tired?" and watch the guy dig for an answer! If your questions are outlandish enough, he will start to freak out and you get to see the real person. It's much easier to deal with this guy as he will have compassion and empathy. Hit him with personal questions like, "Tell me, what is the worst experience you have had with a customer?" or "Are you the top salesman in this yard or is there someone better?" and the training book goes out the window.

Once you have created the instability in the sales presentation (which is usually one-way, he generally asks questions only to elicit information to help his close) you can turn this into a 2-way interaction. At this point, it is no longer a sales interview, it is now a negotiation and you have positioned yourself as an equal. Be aware, this person still has more knowledge on the vehicle, so they can re-introduce this to leverage their position as one of authority, but essentially, you can dismiss this by simply saying, "Let's set aside the car for a moment and focus on the deal". Now the control is yours.

So, what does selling cars have to do with marketing trends? As it turns out, quite a lot! One of the biggest game-changers for sales and marketing in the past 50 years has been the advent and ease of the internet. As a medium, this has become a very non-threatening way of gathering information on an item or service you wish to purchase. Often people wander into car yards with no intention of buying a car – they are there to gather information on a future intention, but the sales scripts are designed to make you get emotionally attached and make a decision now. This effectively turns lookers into buyers.

The internet is a very intuitive method of engaging with lookers. Although you may not be able to (or want to) pressure them into becoming buyers, what you are able to do is to become their source of information on the type of product or service you offer. If you become the prime source for prospective buyers' "how to buy the best widget" information, there are two potential advantages for you. The first is that the prospect is learning is from you (and is possibly focused on your features and benefits). The second is that as people subscribe to your regular material on "how to buy" they will become more confident sooner and will generally make their decision within a shorter time.

So finding and engaging with qualified prospective buyers is the key to increasing the number of prospects and thereby, your number of sales. For most sellers, this could represent a completely new sales channel (place or method of getting sales) and can grow a business rapidly. On the downside, there are sellers out there who set pricing much lower for the same goods and services that they also offer in-store, based on their in-store sales having covered the fixed cost for the business. In economic terms, this is called marginal-cost pricing. This is not a healthy practice for services or goods that are capable of being consumed within your current territory, as it could cannibalise your clientele as they discover they can buy it cheaper online.

Adding sales channels to your business is a far more profitable (and cheaper) way of increasing sales, than opening new operations or outlets. Channel expansion is one of the primary selection criteria that we use to assess a business for value, when a client asks for a due diligence profile (in readiness for purchasing the business). Simply put, a sales channel is a way in which a company supplies its products or services to customers.

I know a clever lady with a cleaning business who has a number of close relationships with real estate companies and who effectively play the role of channels for her cleaners. Frequent end of lease engagements provide plenty of work at better margins than residential work. Her time is better spent in maintaining her channels than in chasing customers.

In my own industry, I have a competitor who has no qualifications and little experience in management consulting, but is consistently one of the highest fee-earners in our industry. On investigation, we discovered that his success was directly related to the fact that he was "first on the scene" when people started their search for business help. He had engaged with some of the best copywriters in Australia and he was able to generate a significant number of inquiries for business consulting services on the basis of online channels.

His conversion was not so hot. He was able to recruit smaller business owners into his "herd" but was less successful with business owners who had experience with consultants, or knew what they wanted to achieve. This evolved into a niche of offering courses in saving or selling your business, for first-time seekers of help. As people used his services and learned how they should measure outcomes to expectations, they drifted off to more experienced consultants for more in-depth engagements. He didn't mind this and simply expanded his promotional reach to other cities and eventually country areas, to maintain the number of enquiries from inexperienced users of consulting services.

This management consultant was successful because he was first in front of buyers through his online channels backed by clever copywriting and professionally structured websites and email promotions. He wasn't the best and he most probably never will be. However, you don't necessarily have to be the best (product or service) in any field to be successful in business if you can simply acquire the customer first.

The Sales Funnel

The most cost-effective method of increasing the value of a business is through sales. Assuming all other factors remain the same, doubling the sales should more than double your net earnings (referred to as the bottom-line). The reason for the increase being more than double, is because you have your fixed costs covered and in most cases, your suppliers may be willing to give you a better buy-price on higher volumes.

So, what is the easiest way to know how to increase (or double) sales? Firstly, you need to understand your sales process, which is sometimes referred to as the sales funnel. This breaks down your business process into stages and we look at where and why we lose prospective buyers or repeat buyers, at each or any stage of the process. We can also then look to how we can add more prospects into the sales funnel, at different stages of the process. A third method is to look for strategic acquisitions that could feed qualified prospects into your sales funnel, with a pre-qualification (if you buy X, you may also need to have Y).

So what is a typical sales funnel? Let me provide one for a service-based industry, as well as a product-based industry. There are thousands of variants for each, but most readers will be able to map their sales funnel from these examples. The first example I use is that of a real estate agency. For this to make sense, one must realise that the sales function for an agent is not selling houses – it is obtaining listings. The more listings they advertise, the more sales they get.

First level: This includes such sources as window displays, walk-ins, repeat buyers, referrals, home-opens, door-knocking, real estate websites, house website, newspapers, keyword advertising, newspaper advertising, rental property owners and direct mail. The outcome is to qualify the opportunities to a point where the representative can get an appointment with the home-owner, to determine if they can help each other.

Second Level: These opportunities are contacted and one or more of three things happen. They get a home visit by the representative for either a casual presentation of services or a preliminary assessment of value. The outcome for this meeting is to obtain approval to value the property and then prepare a presentation, for the home-owner.

Third Level: The next touch-point is the in-home valuation and/or presentation. This can be one or two visits, depending on the skill of the representative. The outcome for this is a listing.

Fourth Level: The final level is the sale and settlement of the property. In some cases, as a vendor's property is sold, that home-owner becomes a prospective buyer. This stage still requires careful management as the level of anxiety during this decision process (for both buyer and seller) is up there with public speaking and death of a loved-one.

Once real estate agency managers understand their sales funnel (and the above is not a definitive list) they are well positioned to start calculating the value of increasing any single variable in their sales funnel and the impact this will have on their bottom line. For instance, if any individual rep's conversion from presentations to listings is 50%, then some investment in negotiating skills will yield substantial dividends, if he is able to increase that to just 60%. This would be a 20% increase in earnings and no additional business or marketing resources required.

When this sales funnel process is fully understood, the principal can start the incremental improvement process by changing one variable at a time and measuring the impact on net earnings. This sales funnel process is not the change catalyst, it is merely a strong indication of where the changes are needed and will do the most good.

Testing Additional Channels

Channels are pathways to your market, and the more channels you have as a rule, the less vulnerable your business could be to competitors. Most businesses have several channels to access their markets. For example, a business may sell directly to customers and indirectly through other industry players. As an example, an automotive repair centre may install a wheel alignment bay and then offer wholesale wheel alignment services to other service centres in the area. This provides a separate channel of wholesale business (to competitors' customers) at a discount rate, but will enable him to keep the equipment working at capacity while he builds up a client base for wheel alignment services.

One of the most sensible channels to add is the Internet. To qualify this one must understand that their product or service must lend itself to being delivered to internet buyers. e.g. If you have a lawn-mowing round, you should only promote this to a handful of post codes – anything more is just noise.

Whatever business you are in, chances are that there is an inundation of offers on the internet for similar services in your territory and for much less than you offer. So what is the best way to be seen above the noise? This is where a good copywriter is essential. All of the language you use might not be the language your buyers use, but a good copywriter will tap into what they are thinking and what makes them hurt or angry and he will develop a series of key words that should be used in any advertising that you put forward.

These key words are generally more effective when they are used to educate the reader in his search for "how to buy ..." You will often see Google ads and other banner advertising offering you "what to look for when buying..." or "what the agents don't want you to know about buying properties..." etc. Another favourite is lists, such as " the top 7 reasons why you should..." and "the 4 food groups you should avoid..."

If you click on these advertisements they provide you with information on how to buy what it is you are gathering information on. If you find one source resonates with you, you may sign up to receive more or regular information from that source. This starts your learning journey with that supplier. Their core objective is to have you reach a buying decision point far earlier than you otherwise would (as you could, if you have the appropriate information) and also to buy from them. After all, they have become a trusted and credible source of your buying decision process; surely it is safer to buy from them?

So to summarise this channel, clever people don't try to sell on the internet, they inform. They offer information to people who seek to increase their own knowledge on how to buy certain goods and services. Ultimately, they will have a host of prospective buyers learning from them, how they should go about buying goods or services. With a sign-up page and a regular newsletter you also have a list of qualified buyers or users, who are more likely to respond to any special offers you have.

So what about selling services on the internet? This can be an excellent tool for engaging and informing your existing regular clients, as well as increasing their frequency of buying, with special offers to bring them back in earlier than their usual cycle.

Another potentially profitable channel through which to increase sales is the 'strategic alliance.' Strategic alliances work where two organisations which offer products or services to the same target market create an alliance which allows them to promote each other's products or services to their respective customers. There is usually a synergy between the services of the two businesses and yet they are separate and distinct. For example when running my capital raising firm in Sydney I would have strategic alliances with accountants, IP lawyers and other business consultants in order to source my clients; the majority of my clients came through these relationships.

Making Every Sales Presentation More Valuable

One of the key strategic boosts for sales is to engage as many as possible one-to-many sales opportunities (such as networking and industry presentations) as well as to engage with opportunities that can generate on-going repeat business. Both of these increase the value of the new client and decrease the opportunity cost of winning a new client.

One of the most underrated methods of generating the one-to-many sales opportunities is through business networking. There are many business networking groups (local and global) which encourage you to present your business opportunity to their members, if you in turn are prepared to watch the individual presentations of other members.

Joining industry groups may be a good way of learning about your industry, but a poor sales channel; selling to your competitors. However, if your business is looking to sell a book of customers who are not perfectly aligned to your core business, then an industry association is the perfect conduit. However, for recruitment of customers, you may be better off joining the local chapter of community groups or their chamber of commerce.

Irrespective of which of these pathways (to engage a greater numbers of 'prospects') you favour, it really pays to get good at the process of selling. Many people misunderstand this process and perform a pushy exercise in persuasion with the result that they have no success. Success in sales is greatly dependent upon being a good listener. I remember one of my early mentors in selling high end consulting services saying to me, "Mate, selling is not telling; you have two ears and one mouth, use them in that proportion."

Once I understood this subtle clue I never looked back in selling and began to enjoy the process. The process is one which allows you to develop better familiarity with the prospect and their problems; problems which you can help solve, thus becoming their champion.

Introduce yourself: This happens at the beginning of all human interactions with someone you are unfamiliar with. Make sure you smile and make the right impression immediately, as first impressions usually last.

Establish rapport: It's true that similarities forge bonds, so quickly determine what you have in common with the person. The quicker you can ask questions about their lives and find commonalities between you and them, the more natural the selling process will be. People more easily buy from those they can identify with.

Identify their needs: Find out what their primary or immediate need is; what is their problem and where is their pain? The number of rejections you have to endure in the selling process is inversely proportional to how well you have established their needs. The better you have identified their needs the deeper and broader is your opportunity to sell (and help them); this is done by asking questions and listening.

Confirm their needs: Ensure that you have established their real needs by repeating back to them and seek agreement that 'these are in fact your real needs.' Don't assume you know. Seeking this clarification tells them that it is important to you that you get it right.

Offer value: Provide solutions specific to their problems by offering value that they cannot refuse. Show that you have understood their problem by demonstrating value in their terms. If they don't want what you offer you just haven't demonstrated enough value. If there is enough value there they will find the money.

Close: 'Closing' is not an exercise in arm-twisting and manipulation but rather a natural progression from offering solutions to their agreed issues and needs. Once there is agreement that the offer is what they want, you simply need to set some action which formalises the sale. Be specific: "We just need to get your credit card details…,"

"Grab your signature…," "Set a time for the kick-off meeting…", "Process your application…", or whatever is the initiating act.

Provide service: Whether it is a service you are selling or not there is 'service' involved. Make sure it is a great experience for your customer to the extent that they give you testimonials and referrals.

The art of selling requires good listening skills and linking your products or services to the values of the customer. Communicating your value is critical and if you can do it genuinely, from the heart with a real want to help the customer you will find the selling process enjoyable; it is the process of helping people.

Tendering

One of the other key strategic boosts for sales is to engage with government or large corporations. This is usually done through a tendering system and can be quite a lucrative way of gaining contracts for supply or service.

Although the more generic goods and services contracts do not provide significant margins, your presence as an approved supplier can provide you with access to these government and large corporate buyers for non-tenured equipment and services beyond the scope of the supply contract, once you have established a relationship with the key personnel.

The other key advantage is the increased volume of equipment you will be selling. This will increase your volume from your supplier and may take you to a higher price break. This is more prevalent in government supply, where most computer forms have "Education and Government" buy prices for agencies, which you can then buy all of your needs through. This will effectively reduce your buy price and increase your margins to all of your regular customers, making you more competitive in your space.

However, tendering is fickle and requires a high level of compliance to be included onto the shortlist. If you do not provide an adequate response on your critical criteria, you may be excluded from the shortlist without any opportunity to amend. This can be despite your being substantially better value to the client. The good news is that there are plenty of grant-writers and tender writers who can prepare the documentation for you that will guarantee your compliance. The bad news is that they bill you regardless of your success. Overall, it is well worth getting someone to do your first major tender and then using this as a template for future tenders, if you are on a budget.

It is wise to build a tender database if you are intending to submit tenders regularly in future in that much of the information from previous tenders may be relevant to future tenders. Every tender you submit should evolve your level of refinement in the time and quality of your submissions. A 'knowledge base' which houses all your key submissions and important tender information can save you a lot of time, allowing you to focus on the critical parts of the tender and ultimately win you a lot more work.

It is also worth mentioning that winning tenders, like other means of acquiring work, can be enormously enhanced by having relationships with the key people within the client organisation. Too many smaller businesses rely on the submission of the tender document to win them the work when in reality the business which wins the work is the one which has the strongest relationship with the organisation putting the tender out. Understand who the organisations are that you would like to successfully submit a bid to in the future and put together a schedule of meeting their key decision makers and influencers.

Your Online Opportunities

The most underrated new channel opportunity for most small businesses can be the internet. We understand that people make fortunes on the internet every day, but we generally have trouble relating this to our businesses or to our town or city. It does happen. It is sometimes accidental, but usually it is the result of some very clever construction by people who know this space.

The elements we need to accelerate our business activity on the internet include (1) Great copywriting, (2) A clean and understandable website structure, (3) A compelling offer to engage people – not necessarily sell them anything immediately, and (an automated systems that will capture, process and disperse information that will not require us to spend our day answering email enquiries or sending prices to people we cannot service.

Let me save you some time. If you spend 2 weeks to 4 years studying web marketing, SEO and other internet tools, the prime lesson you will learn is that there are people who are already experts in providing these services and you need to engage the good ones before your competitors do.

They are not hard to find and because their businesses are internet-based, they can be found easily. When you find some specialists with the right credentials, you will need to investigate these carefully, ensuring that you ask for a list of referees and then you make direct contact with them, (not by email – they may just be sites they created) and make your selection based on their track record, not on the look and feel of some sites. There is no guarantee that your tastes and preferences reflect those customers who do or could buy from you.

Of all the growth requirements in our book, the website, copywriting and search engine optimisation are the three areas where we recommend you outsource, as the learning is too long and can be too costly. However, do not set this aside as it can be a very lucrative method of building your client base from areas you otherwise could not access.

As a pertinent example, we wanted to present our Formula 1 coaching program to the Western Australian small-to-medium enterprise market, to help them double their net earnings in a ten-month engagement, using our affordable, clustered consulting model. We had a very compelling offer and guaranteed our services, but we didn't want to offer this to our regular client base, as these were companies with a $5m plus turnover.

We tried to do this ourselves. We studied, learned, practiced and eventually engaged friends, to get the message out there. Our first workshop got half of the expected bookings and a full 50% of these didn't show! We knew we had to change.

We finally identified the experts in our field and the people who provided services to our more successful peers (some of whom had no sound message but still did better than us!). We learned from these people, with the fundamental message being to get the best help, get coaching to round out your weaknesses and outsource the stuff that you need to. End of problem.

Increasing your sales is generally the greatest challenge in business. Remember that increasing sales starts with increasing the number customers which is a function of increasing the number of 'leads' your business attracts multiplied by the 'conversion rate.' There are many mechanisms, strategies and skills by which you may increase the leads and conversion rate for your business and it really requires some careful thought and understanding of your customer to know what is the right combination for your business.

The most successful businesses are usually the ones which continuously attract customers in the numbers and of the type they want. Make sure you develop the right strategies, allocate the right resources and always test and measure this most critical endeavour to increase sales.

How do we continually attract the right prospects?

It stands to reason that if we needed to double our number of customers, we could simply double our promotional budget or our promotional activities. This doesn't exactly work that well, due to a number of factors (economists call it the law of diminishing marginal returns). There are ways of working smarter for the average small business that do not cost a fortune or commit you to long-term campaigns or programs to achieve your increase objectives.

The most effective three-step program to increase the number of qualified prospective buyers is to follow these three simple steps:

You will firstly need to segment all existing and past buyers into Category A, B or C clients. Category B clients are the ideal clients we would be happy to attract more of. Category A clients are advocates who bring us new customers by influencing others to buy and category C clients cost us most (if not all) of our margins.

Your second step is to conduct an informal focus-group session with a small sample of As and Bs and find out what they liked about your service or products, what was the key reason they purchased from you and also what motivated them to take action and make a purchase in the first place. This should be done independently of the company, by an un-related party (marketing departments of most universities have postgraduate students requiring experience in focus group facilitation).

Once you have identified the practical and logical motivations for buyers, you need to find the emotional reasons. Understanding what makes them angry about your industry, the buying process or the application they have for your product or service will help you prepare your messages to them with far greater precision, to have a fraction of the additional B profile clients to effectively double your sales. We eventually use this information in advertising, online search engines and other areas in which our prospective B-class clients are looking, to search for information on our favourite topic – our business.

Your final step is to convert your C-class clients to B-class clients, or drive them to your competitors. If one client is costing you more of your time than any other and is not obtaining or recognising the value you offer him, you need to make the level of service equal to the amount you charge him. If they require twice the service activity to sell, deliver, install (or otherwise provide a product or service) than your average B-class client, then the most effective method could be pricing.

Through decades of evaluating and re-prioritising problem customers for our clients, we developed a process called FOPs. This acronym refers to Fxxx Off Pricing, in which we increase the prices for their products or services (or in some cases we have increased everybody's prices and offered exclusive rebates to the B and A-class clients) so that the cost of providing the product or service to these clients will then classify them as C-class clients.

What usually happens in these cases is that they walk away and although most small business owners are initially upset by this, they very quickly recognise the high level of resources the C-class client was using, which is now freed up for more B-class clients.

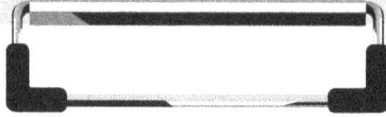

SUMMARY NOTES

☑ The sales funnel concept is an easy-to-understand process for sales, from prospects to customers.

☑ Additional channels are discussed, including tendering and the internet.

☑ Attracting the right customers is easier if you fully understand what the right customers want to buy, where and how.

☑ It is prudent to periodically classify clients to determine which group is making and/or costing you money.

CHAPTER 8
'The Team' – The Importance and Function of Your Crew

"Outstanding leaders go out of their way to boost the self esteem of their personnel. If people believe in themselves, it's amazing what they can accomplish."

Sam Walton
(Founder of Walmart)

CHAPTER 8

'THE TEAM' – THE IMPORTANCE AND FUNCTION OF YOUR CREW

It is often said that the challenges presented by 'people' to a small or fast-growing business owner, are second only to the challenges associated with winning enough work. Any way you look at it, unless you have a completely automated online business, it is inevitable that you will be confronted with the challenge of managing the 'people problem.' Your people are the key to providing you with leverage and freedom and representing your good name out in the marketplace, so it is imperative that you get your team right.

So frequently, owners of small to medium business are not fully appreciative of the critical importance that their people play in the overall success (or failure) of their business. Many will seek to save money on employing someone who is going to be cheaper than the rest, but is not skilled or experienced enough in a given role. Others don't provide the training and guidance to develop the person's capacity to do the job and then complain that the person is not performing well enough. This is a recipe for disaster. Don't let this be you. Remember that your people set the tone for your organisation; they are, as the old cliché says, 'your most valuable resource.'

As a general rule, never speculate on whether someone can 'do the job' and then fail to provide enough support and guidance in doing the job. It is always better to err on the side of employing someone who can clearly demonstrate from past experience that they can do what is required and you should provide more guidance, training and support to ensure that the job gets done really well.

The process of forming a winning team starts at the point of determining the required organisational structure. It continues through the role definition and recruitment phases before setting people up for success in their job, getting employees fully engaged in their roles, making sure you keep these people and developing leaders from within. Each of these stages is critical to the success of the business and demands the right level of focus, commitment and action.

Strategic Planning for Your People Needs

The first stage in building a winning and cohesive team requires an overall perspective on what roles need to be played in delivering the business objectives and the relationship between these roles. An 'Organisational Structure' needs to be devised for the immediate needs of the organisation in delivering strategy and thought should always be given to how this structure will alter over time, as the business matures and as strategic objectives are met.

Typically, a business will start with a flat structure where the 'driver' is responsible for many of the key functional areas; these functional areas would include 'Management and Administration, 'Finance and Accounting', 'Marketing and Sales', 'R & D', 'Operations and Delivery' and 'Human Resources.' However, as the business evolves and matures, people are acquired to take on management of these different functional divisions. Usually the first step in the process of evolving the structure is the strategic recruitment of personnel to perform the administrative tasks associated with business generally so that the driver can transition from an operational role to a management role.

The types of staff that are required should always be closely related to the strategy of the business which of course is geared to achieving the vision. The acquisition of key personnel is a strategic exercise itself and great thought should be dedicated to identifying 'when' various staff are to be brought into the organisation and identifying what set of circumstances need to prevail before making the appointment. This should be identified to determine the trigger for 'when' a given appointment should occur.

This should also factor in the financial cost and the financial gains, in the short and long term. There are sometimes situations where the recruitment, induction, training and placement of the key person might not be expected to yield an immediate return (such as with a professional practice, which needs to take on more appointments to fill the additional capacity).

The organisational structure should be viewed as the relationship between the various roles to ensure that all the necessary tasks in the business are being grouped and managed in the most effective way. This will ensure that each role covers all the relevant ground without an overlap of tasking, reporting or planning. Well-defined job roles come from a strong understanding of the work processes to be performed in a given functional space and are critical in getting things done in the most efficient manner.

When you have the appropriate structure in place and you have job descriptions for each position (regardless of whether these positions are vacant, filled or presently occupied by you, the driver) you need to find the right people.

Acquiring the Right People

Job Descriptions

The challenge of attracting and acquiring good people for your business starts with a well-constructed job description. This document needs to provide an accurate reflection of the duties, responsibilities, accountabilities, as well as the required skills and experience, the job and the expectations associated with it. The job description provides a reference point from which to manage the process of acquiring staff. Beyond the recruitment phase, this provides a first tool for managing performance.

Typically, the job description will consist firstly of a couple of paragraphs describing the role, then the 'duties and responsibilities,' then the necessary 'skills and qualifications' before specifying the KPI's (key performance indicators). I intend to discuss KPI's a little later in the chapter.

Conditions such as annual leave, working hours and the like should also be stated and finally there should be a section for the employee to sign acknowledgement of having received and understood the job description. The resources of the Formula 1 for Business website gives you a range of job description templates.

Employing someone without a job description can be destructive to your organisation, as it sets everyone up for disappointment. The clearer the expectations of the role, set at the beginning of the engagement, the more likely that the person entering the role will be successful.

You would be surprised at how often people are employed without a job description. Usually in these cases the employer has the gall to blame the employee when things don't work out when really the guy they should be asking questions of is the guy looking back at them in the mirror.

Another critical error is to ask the personnel in the position to create or amend their own job description. Firstly, if a person is asked to outline how they could or should be judged within their role, there is no real incentive there for them to aim for anything at or beyond mediocrity. If they consider their capacity to pay their mortgages will hinge on their ability to achieve the requirements in this job description, you are not going to see any accountabilities or strategic growth, are you?

Recruiting

Once the job has been defined, the challenge of actually recruiting is the next critical phase. The fight for talent over an increasing scarcity of specific skills through the last few years has made the task of recruitment all the more important. Gone are the days of simply running an advert in the local newspaper and having a bunch of qualified candidates respond. The balance of power has swung around in favour of the skilled employee and I have often heard clients gripe that when they interview someone (particularly from generation Y) for a job they often feel like they are the one being interviewed.

Over the past thirty years, the recruitment industry has evolved to provide services to businesses needing help in finding the staff they need, however they are not widely used by small to medium enterprises due to their perceived cost. It is possible to source good candidates yourself however, if you are having a hard time getting the right person for an important role it may be worth the money to get an agency to fill the role successfully. It can become a more expensive use of your time, finding the right candidate or worse still, a very expensive exercise employing the wrong person and potentially having to do it all again when they don't work out. The focus should always be on getting the right person and with agency guarantees, this will become a more promising proposition.

You can source candidates online through advertising on seek.com or by using social media such as LinkedIn and Facebook. LinkedIn is good as you can identify groups with particular skill-sets. In fact many of the recruitment firms use LinkedIn to source specialist candidates.

Leave nothing to chance when going through the process of hiring people for your team. You may have heard the old saying, 'hire slow and fire fast.' Once you have employed someone they are 'in' and getting rid of them and doing it all again is all too costly in terms of time, money, efficiency and morale so you really need to get it right (I'll get to the 'firing fast' bit later).

When preparing to interview candidates understand the content of their resume and mark questions on it where you would like explanation or more information. For example: "So I see you left X company, why was that?" Also design a number of open questions relevant to the job which they cannot answer 'yes' or 'no' to, so that you get them talking and providing real information. You need the real story and it's too late after you have made the appointment. Open questions might start with, 'Tell me about a time when you...,' or 'Give me an example of...,' or 'Describe...' There are some off-the-shelf job description packages which provide interview questions for the hirers. These are not expensive and could save you a small fortune in litigation and payout fees.

We caution you on the legislation relating to personal, family and other questions (such as religious, sexual orientation, etc.) but we do encourage you to invent creative questions that will invoke an emotional response. This may break the applicant's well-rehearsed façade and allow you (sometimes just for an instant) to see the real person that you will need to deal with.

It also pays when preparing for interviews, particularly when talking with people who may have multiple options, to develop a 'Unique Selling Proposition' for your business. This ensures that you are able to position your business in the best possible light; almost like you would do for customers but designed to 'sell' the business to the best candidates. For example, I have a number of clients who would lose potentially good staff to the mining industry because it pays more, but after we developed a 'USP' for staff clearly identifying benefits of 'working for us' instead of mining, there was an immediate improvement in recruitment success.

After initial introductions in the interview, ask them what attracted them to the job. Then give a brief introduction to the history and the structure of the business. Introduce them to the job description and give them an opportunity to ask questions about the role before going through their resume and asking the questions you marked on it earlier. Then ask the specific open questions you prepared. After you have noted everything important in their responses give them an opportunity to ask any question they may have before finishing the interview by taking them through what the rest of the recruitment and selection process will be.

Reference Checking

So you now have someone you think can fill the role. The next step is to conduct reference checks - never omit this step. Talk to those they have nominated as referees with prepared, structured questions and talk with others you may know who have had any dealings with them who are not referees. Talk to at least four referees.

Ask their referees if there is anyone else you should talk to. It amazes me when an employer does not do adequate reference checks and then is surprised and disappointed when their new employee is not all that they hoped for.

Do not rely on email interviews, as you may actually be communicating with the candidate! Always make a time to call them and ask for their main telephone switchboard number, so you can confirm they are from the firm they say they are. I am reminded of the beginnings of a now global computer company, which started its existence in the early 1980's, in Kaohsiung (southern Taiwan) as an electronics components supplier to some computer companies. The four partners wanted to start an assembly plant themselves but couldn't break into the business. They eventually submitted a tender for a USA national government department and were shortlisted for the supply of tens of thousands of computers per month.

One of the tender pre-conditions was that they were to be inspected by the tender board nominee. They had no plant to inspect, but they did have clients with computer assembly plants, who had building signs in Mandarin and no English. These enterprising partners asked their client if they could bring some Americans through, to see how that plant used the components they supplied. The Taiwanese company agreed and these partners made a visit the day before and got to know the staff and supervisors.

On the day of the inspection, they collected the nominee from his hotel by limousine and pulled up at the rear entrance of the factory. They walked him through and chatted (in Chinese) to all of the people they "knew" and then had him back at the hotel in time for a good lunch. They got the deal and were still one of the largest computer suppliers to the USA Government well into the 1990's. Although this company was able to get their act together and deliver on their empty promises, this situation had the potential of going horribly wrong for the buyer. A similar situation can easily be orchestrated by applicants for jobs they are keen to get.

Remuneration

Pay people well. If you want good people offer them the respect that they deserve by paying them well and you will discover that you make your money back twofold by the job being done well and the other positive benefits to the business associated with having 'better' rather than 'lesser' staff. We have all heard of the saying, 'If you pay peanuts you get monkeys.'

I have known of some terrible appointments where a business manager has placed people in important roles for which they do not have all the necessary skills because he wanted to save some money. Taking this option usually provides a steep haul up a more expensive path. Usually in this scenario the new employee is not given the additional support, training or mentoring they need and the effects of their resulting poor performance is not confined only to their role, rather it negatively impacts on other staff, the business efficiency and worst case, the customers. In some cases, other staff leave before the problem is identified and rectified. There should be no shortcuts here, pay the right candidate the right money and get the right result.

Character

For the final word on acquiring good staff, let me offer you this. If in the process of recruitment and selection, you are faced with the option of choosing according to 'skills' or 'character' always err on side of 'character.' Obviously a certain amount of skill and experience is required to perform the fundamental duties of any given job but if one candidate has an outstanding character but fewer skills than another it is likely that these skills can quickly be acquired.

The reverse however, does not apply as character is not as easily acquired as a skill. If a person has demonstrated in their background, an ability to overcome obstacles, persist in the face of discouragement, be creative, innovate, take responsibility, communicate and build relationships they are likely to be able to grow into the skills part of the role and provide many other benefits due to their character. They are also likely to have a greater positive effect on and relationships with other staff. Never underestimate the significance of character.

Setting People Up For Success

Having taken on a new employee it is important that they feel comfortable in their new role, have adequate support and are brought up to speed as soon as possible so that they are able to perform most of their role competently. There is nothing more deflating for someone starting a new job than to have their natural enthusiasm and hopes for their new role, dashed by bad preparation for them starting. We all like to be useful and acknowledged, but if the planning or circumstances do not allow it, this could affect the candidate for years.

Make sure you have a well-structured induction program ready for them which will introduce them to everything and everybody in the business whom they need to know. An induction program should take them through the systems and processes they need to use to do their job properly and provide the necessary grounding and resources to provide confidence to the new employee and management and ensure that they will succeed in their new role. The most important part of any induction is the vision, mission and values of the company, which they are inevitably going to be asked to live by during working hours.

It can also be a good move to provide a 'mentor' relationship to new employees who can provide direction and guidance. Sure, in smaller businesses it may be hard to have someone perform this role who is not the direct superior, but if there is an opportunity this role can become a positive thing for everyone concerned. Be prepared to be asked by a well-mentored candidate, if that person can take on the mentorship role in the future.

Getting People Engaged

A real problem in a lot of workplaces is that employees are just not engaged. By engaged I mean giving their best, being energised, focused, involved and motivated to being a part of the business and doing as well as they can. Now I'm not talking about some altruistic ideal where everyone meditates and sings songs together at lunch time, I mean linking the healthy self-interests of individual employees to the greater good of the organisation.

One of the most effective methods of enabling this is to offer all personnel a customised and structured course in personal goal-setting. We have provided some goal-setting information in earlier chapters, but would encourage business owners to have a structured course prepared for their personnel, to ensure genuine and lasting alignment of personal and business goals.

When people can be shown how to align their personal goals with their corporate goals, you will never need to motivate these people again. In the 1990's, I was challenged by one of my peers (in a postgraduate

workshop) to try an experiment which I was later able to implement in Perth when I returned. This was not easy, but I was lucky enough to have all of the pieces fall into place and I was working with a very understanding client, who gave me the freedom to achieve this. He has no regrets.

The client was a large printing organisation. Competition was very severe, in a declining market (boutique printing franchises were starting to pop up everywhere) and this firm was looking to motivate their senior sales person to start achieving the sales they knew he was capable of. We interviewed him off-site and identified that in his vision of the most successful senior sales person would be one of the most prominent features, a Fairlane car. As it turned out, his competitor had a sales manager who was driving such a car and this guy only had a Falcon (the cheaper version of the same vehicle).

Now the first thing we know is that this poor guy is losing sales in only one area – between his ears. However, we assessed that he may not be able to see this, so we designed a program that could transition him into a fully-featured version of the Fairlane, which was probably going to be better than his competitor. The program required an extra $40,000 in sales per month, with the same or better margins. To achieve this, we calculated the number of sales, new customers, repeat volumes, sales calls, and contacts he had to generate in a month. This came down to one critical requirement - he needed to make an extra four telephone calls per day, based on his current sales presentation and closing ratios!

The manager did not believe this would work, but reached out with a promise. If the guy achieved his target for three straight months he could order the car, but if he fell below this target, he could expect to swap this car with another member of staff (who was still driving the more modest falcon).

The problem this guy had was clearly all in his head. Our goal-setting plan aligned his goals with the company goals and there was no need to motivate him again. He was clearly the better salesman, as his vehicle reflected that to all of his clients (but more importantly, to his perception of himself).

Vision and Development Path

We believe there are two key principles behind getting people engaged in their work to maximise their contribution to a business. The first principle is based on helping the employee build their own personal vision and helping them move towards this vision of theirs with a 'development path.' This starts right at the point of interview and entry into the organisation when you start to identify a person's desired future with open questions such as, 'So where do you want to go in life?' or 'Where do you want to be in ten years?'

Having a good understanding of where your people want to go, will give you the privileged position of potentially being able to help them walk that path. If they have no idea of where they want to go then you are in a position to help them build their vision. Either way, the discussion of their vision and an earnest endeavour to help set them in that direction will definitely build a stronger relationship with them and have them more receptive to your vision and their place in helping you achieve it. Together you can build a vision for their progression in skills and capacity through working in your business.

When you can position in their mind their role in your business as a mutually beneficial relationship which helps you both get what you want and you will do whatever you can to help each other, you are setting the footing for a very positive relationship. Beyond just identifying their vision, you must then build their 'development path' together.

The development path is essentially the skills and experiences they wish to acquire that you can facilitate as part of or related to the work they are doing in your business. It may involve formal training, informal mentoring, up-skilling on the job or external activities but it must be structured and measured. As in relationships of any kind, the more you can help the other party get what they want, the more they will help you get what you want. The second key principle we believe sits behind employee engagement and is recognition.

Recognition, Reward and Incentive

Everyone loves to be recognised and rewarded for a job well done. In the workplace it is often assumed that these things are necessarily associated with more money. Research consistently shows that more money is not a substitute for good, old fashioned appreciation and some recognition in front of peers. Simply voicing your appreciation goes a long way with another human being: "That was a great job you did yesterday Tom, well done."

This is an easy thing to do, it costs you nothing and it makes for a positive environment in the workplace where people will strive to do things which will draw more positive affirmation because it feels good. Look for any opportunity to recognise and congratulate people for doing a good job.

There can also be more a formal means of giving incentives and rewarding staff and there are many models for doing this according to the nature of the business and roles within it. Incentives can be individually or team based and are generally monetary; they must be associated with KPI's and performance. For small to medium sized businesses it is often best to begin this process with a 'profit share' arrangement whereby the business distributes a certain portion of profit to teams or individuals according to their performance when profitability goes beyond a certain level.

Rewarding employees for their efforts can also be non-monetary and not necessarily part of their conditions of employment (as incentives are). When someone has done a good job you may reward them with a voucher for a product, tickets to an event or possibly some special privilege – anything that they will appreciate. Rewards for your team are only as limited as the imagination but you can be confident that if you do first recognise people and then reward them, they will be more engaged in performing their role.

The fight to firstly secure good employees and the work required to get them engaged is all necessary to developing and keeping the talent which is the key to building your business successfully. Once you have got people up to speed and contributing their talents, your objective should be to keep these people and that means constantly providing them with the stimulation, recognition and reward for them to be satisfied.

Culture of Inclusion and Continuous Improvement

Over many years we have observed that the most successful businesses, large and small, have a culture of inclusion and continuous improvement. Inclusion simply means ensuring that employees are informed, given a chance to contribute their views, are genuinely listened to and are made to feel that they belong.

The first basic step to developing a culture of inclusion is to have a business wide monthly meeting where information is shared with all the employees at the same time and they are given an opportunity to interact in a forum that represents the business. This can be held at lunch time or at the end of the day and is used to communicate information to staff about what is happening in and around the company. These things may include: What changes are happening, what is being done well, what is being done not so well, who is being recognised and rewarded this month, new sales or contracts won, celebrations of success and any newsworthy information.

People like being included and when you think of the alternative, the results are not palatable: Rumours circulating, divisions and rifts between different parts of the business, speculation and uncertainty. A monthly get together is a necessary means of bringing people together to remind them that we are one team pulling for a common cause. It also provides a forum where employees can contribute their views.

Continuous improvement in any organisation is important and monthly meetings can be an effective means of bringing to light opportunities for improvement. Depending on the size of the business, continuous improvement can either be the domain of a divisional or company wide meeting. The important thing with continuous improvement is that suggested items for improvement are formally logged and acted upon. If there is actual continuous improvement through employee suggestion then it is a great way for people to get involved by actually seeing that their suggestion is brought to life, however if suggestions are not acted upon you will have a real credibility crisis on your hands.

The reality is that most of the really good improvement suggestions come from the ground floor, where people are actually doing the work so it pays to provide opportunities for employees to contribute their thoughts and to listen; there is gold within those employees.

Your employees are the soul of your organisation and they are the greatest single factor in determining the success or failure of your strategy in the pursuit of your vision. Managing them well is therefore a huge factor in your success as a business owner. Here's a not so little secret: When employee job satisfaction and motivation increases, profitability increases too.

When People Don't Work Out

If you think carefully about people you have been associated with, you might realise that nearly all of these people were "let-go" from at least one position, during the course of their respective careers. This is not necessarily a reflection on the individual, but could simply be the "fit" with the organisation or the team dynamic. There are a number of factors that may necessitate the redundancy of one or more of your personnel from time to time and it is always best to act quickly and decisively. The most essential mandate in this process is to hire carefully and fire quickly.

Some of the steps you should take (after you have taken the necessary steps to comply with the employment regulations in your particular jurisdiction) should include:

Have a prepared statement for this person, a similar one for remaining personnel, a small carton (for personal effects) and a taxi voucher, ready in your office. Have a list of company items this person was entitled to use or carry, in the course of their employment. This may include keys, mobile phone, laptop, etc.

Call the person and ask them to see you in your office. Immediately after this phone call (and prior to the meeting) you should advise the IT department to suspend the persons' login and access codes. You should have an automatic divert on emails set to their immediate superior.

Bring the person into your office or a private area, preferably at the end of the day, when there are fewer of their work colleagues to observe.

Prepare a statement relating to the steps taken, the reasons for the decision and then (with eye-contact) apologise for the inevitable action.

Inform the person of their entitlements and rights and (if the person was entitled to a company vehicle) provide a taxi home for them.

Accompany them to their workstation or office and assist them with the collection of their personal effects.

Accompany them to the front door and wish them well.

Return to your office and immediately send out an email to all personnel advising them of the departure of the person. No reasons need to be given.

It is not imperative, but advisable (particularly for smaller companies) to convene a meeting with all staff who interacted with the person, to explain why they were let go and to allay fears that further dismissals are imminent. It is appropriate to read the prepared statement you have for the dismissal interview and then open the floor for questions. People will need to vent in some cases and depending on the popularity of the individual, there could be some anxiety.

The most critical issue is not to put this person down, in their absence. If that person was dismissed for dishonest dealings or any other issue that could result in legal proceedings, you should not use this as a justification. If it is raised, it might be prudent to point out to the group that every person is entitled to the presumption of innocence and you would rather leave this speculation to the courts or the police.

In conclusion, your people are the source of one of your greatest challenges in business and they also provide the basis for the greatest rewards in your business. If you are successful in recruiting, developing, engaging and keeping good people you will go a long way towards developing a successful and valuable business which will allow you both financial freedom and time.

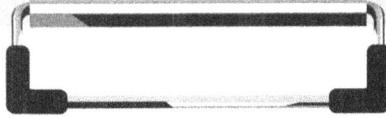

SUMMARY POINTS

☑ Human resource planning and recruitment is a critical task for all small businesses. Poor HR strategies can kill a good business. Care must be taken in selection and quick action is required to terminate where justified.

☑ People management is a lot like parenting. If the kids don't behave appropriately, it is ALWAYS the parents fault. Likewise, inappropriate activity can only manifest itself if the recruitment and/or management process is not functioning well.

☑ Hire slow and fire fast. Always speak to referees and post hypothetical questions that will give better perspectives for you. Ask if they would consider re-hiring the candidate…

☑ Structure your remuneration program so that the base is below average and the bonus will elevate them to above the industry average. If they do not intend to give it 100% they will not earn what they could elsewhere.

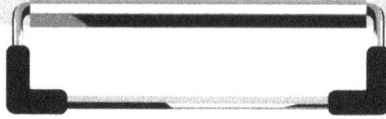

☑ If termination is required, do not hesitate. This chapter provides an 8-step program to terminate with dignity. We don't advocate "trimming the herd to send a message" but if performance is not up to the required standard and all support is being provided, make the decision and push it through.

CHAPTER 9

From Driver to Owner – Working Your Way Out of the Business

"The art of management is the planning, organisation, leadership and control of resources, for a common purpose."

Philip Kotler

CHAPTER 9

FROM DRIVER TO OWNER – WORKING YOUR WAY OUT OF THE BUSINESS

Most businesses start out as an individual with a dream or a vision of what they would like to bring to the world by way of products or services and these products or services are usually things for which this person has skills relevant to or some special knowledge of. This person we will call the 'skilled worker' and they may be any skilled person looking to build a business with those skills providing a foundation for the end product. He may be an accountant, a mechanic, an electrician, a computer technician – you get the picture.

Now as long as this skilled worker is the primary means of delivering the work, he is really still in the position of having a job rather than having a business; sure he doesn't have to report to a boss any more, but if he stops working he stops earning. Many of those in the world of the 'self-employed' suffer this problem and the key to growing beyond it and developing a 'business' is to understand that there are separate and distinct roles within a business, with each having a separate and yet distinctive philosophy, psychology and set of objectives.

What are the Roles?

We have mentioned the 'skilled worker' who starts a business most probably having acquired their skills through a job and then seeks to provide these skills directly to clients himself. The problem with this all too common type of situation is that the skilled worker only has the skills he presently has to build the business into something bigger, so as to allow him some freedom from always having to 'do the work.'

He is restrained by the psychology which he brought from working for someone else where he does the work, does some more work if he is lucky and then looks for more work to do. It doesn't take someone too much time working in this fashion to realise that they are in a trap – similar to a job, in that you are working for money. The upside of not having a boss has the equal or greater downside of not having any paid leave and having to find your own work.

Soon the skilled worker makes the decision to employ other skilled workers to do some of the work so that he has more than a job and can control his destiny to a greater extent by being able to service more clients by not being required to do all of the work. If he is able to delegate the additional work to these incumbents, he then becomes the driver of his business vehicle and is responsible for steering through the maze of opportunities, challenges and problems which constantly confront the person running a business.

However, he has a problem. He was never trained to operate the business, just the functions within the business. He has never acquired the skills and knowledge necessary to discharge the responsibilities associated with the management and administration, and the finance and accounting aspects of the business; the marketing and sales to ensure sufficient customer flow, the human resources to ensure people are acquired, developed and maintained effectively, and of course the smooth driving of operations to make sure work is delivered in the right quality and quantity.

This represents the greatest challenge to the evolution of any small business as the skilled worker recognises that he is in need of help to do what needs to be done in the driving seat. There are a number of different ways people go about doing this. The person more comfortable with sales looks to find an operations person and the person comfortable running operations looks for a sales person.

The hand-off sounds logical and acceptable, but can become very difficult for the business owner. Having performed this service function at a significantly high level for several years as a sole operator, he will inevitably recruit personnel who are less-skilled (and pay them accordingly). The temptation for some is to not allow them to complete their work to their standard.

In a small specialty business we looked at several years ago, the business model was sufficiently unique (and the margins were substantial!) for us to look at expanding the model to operate a separate site in each State and replicate the function through either a shared or franchise model. We set about getting the business owner out of the business so he could be free to design the replica plants for other cities and also to allow us to observe the operators prior to us preparing the job descriptions, KPIs, accountabilities and procedures manual.

We observed some employee dissent, which was revealed as interference. When the consultants were not present, the principal was get frustrated with his employees and pushed them aside and started to complete the tasks himself. As a result they would get frustrated and either leave or argue, which earned them a dismissal. After we interviewed several of these past employees, we got the profile of an "artisan" approach, but for many of these ex-staff there was the perception of a dictator! We eventually did not expand this business and disengaged with the client over a period of weeks, ensuring he was not disadvantaged by his association with our team. We assess that as a failure, as we were not able to change his behaviours, despite his acceptance of this as wrong and his constant promises to change.

Sometimes the person wanting the change process to be managed for him, may elect to select and engage a business coach. This is a big decision for most business owners, as their biggest (or second-biggest) asset is being placed in the hands of a stranger. This process does have inherent risks associated with the history, knowledge, experience and competency of the consultant.

The consultant you may be most comfortable with might have had a hairdressing business two years ago (no disrespect to hairdressers) and purchased a business coaching franchise. This is certainly not besmirching all business coaches however, many of them have neither the knowledge nor the experience to be providing advice of how to successfully run and build value in a business. The driver's primary responsibility is to deliver the strategy of the business to achieve the objectives identified within strategic planning. We will explore the 'drivers seat' question in greater detail, shortly.

The other role not to be overlooked in the landscape of the evolving business is that of the owner. The owner must have a firm grasp of the ultimate vision and objectives of the business in order to set goals for the driver and these will depend on the personal perspectives of the owner. He may wish to sell the business in five years, he may want to develop it as a solid going concern which provides him with passive cash flow or he might want to pass it on to his children. Whatever the case, the owner must understand how the business is going, relative to the strategic plans he developed at the beginning of each planning cycle. He must also have a firm basis upon which to assess the driver's performance and he must be able to understand the financials and the critical success factors of the business.

How Many of these Roles are being Performed by You?

This is a really challenging question for many small business people particularly because they may not fully appreciate the two roles they are less familiar with; Business Driver and Owner. Of course, in answering this question, most small business people will identify themselves rightly as 'being responsible' for these roles, however it is not often that the same respondent can say that they have a firm grip on both the driving and the ownership roles. These are the strategic roles responsible for the long term direction and operational success of the business and they need to be done with clarity, purpose and ability.

Now in revisiting the 'driver's seat' role, the driver should have a sound knowledge of and be involved in all of the things presented up to this chapter. He should play a role in forming and communicating the vision, build the strategic plan, set and monitor the business goals and he should be managing the profit drivers, managing key business numbers and ensuring that sales are expanding, while also building the team's performance and promoting innovation and continuous improvement.

This sure sounds like a lot but when the driver is free to drive and does not have to do any of the work, much of this is taken care of on an ongoing basis after the establishment of systems and processes to deliver the information he needs to drive the business towards its objectives. The external help which is most needed by the majority of small to medium enterprises to assist the driver is in the area of analysing the present state of the business, building an exciting vision for the future and developing strategic plans, goals and measures to provide the driver with a reliable vehicle which he can power to victory. Without the process and the direction, businesses can get lost, irrespective of whether they are large or small. However, with a clear and measurable way forward, and with

processes and systems in place to provide the driver with a 'dashboard' of key information the job of driving becomes easier. The core focus can become driving, with only a limited time required to check the instruments and ensure the entire crew is performing as required.

Having said that, a full and frank assessment of the present 'driving abilities' also needs to be conducted to understand how much assistance or learning is needed to effectively drive the business; after all, it is futile to set the business vehicle up to go much faster if the driver is not comfortable driving at higher speeds. An honest skills audit across the functional areas of the business will tell you which area you will need help with. To refresh your memory these are: Management and Administration, Finance and Accounting, Marketing and Sales, Human Resources and the final one, being R & D, Development and Operations.

Of course selecting where you get your external assistance from is critical to your businesses future. Just like when employing a new team member, examine their past performance and speak to those who have experienced their service. Don't rely on their word or a franchised coaching name to give you assurance of expertise. Also, if you can develop a mentor relationship, either formal and paid or informal and unpaid, this can be of immeasurable value.

How will You get these Hats on Other Heads?

It is generally accepted that a successful business is one where the owner does not work in the business either as a skilled worker or as the driver (and these businesses are worth more as we will discover in the next chapter). So how is it that we set forth on the pathway to being a business owner who is not constrained by the need to work in the business? It all starts with the transition from skilled worker to driver.

Rarely does it involve a jump straight from skilled worker to owner on the basis that the owner needs an appreciation of the driver's seat before he is in a position to understand the driver's performance.

Shifting from skilled worker to driver is largely a matter of successfully recruiting skilled workers to replace yourself as the hub of production in operations, while ensuring that sales continue to increase, and then learning how to drive the business. We examined in some depth back in chapter 7 how to acquire staff and then set them up to win (revisit chapter 7 if you need to).

As the business grows, there will inevitably be a need to acquire staff and skills outside of just the core operational skills. These might include accounting and book keeping, marketing and sales, and specialist HR skills in training and development. Remember that there are increasing opportunities to outsource this work to cost-efficient external alternatives.

As far as shifting from driver to owner and out of the operational machinery of the business, this transition more often requires a careful delegation of duties and gradual development of one or several key skilled workers who may or may not have already demonstrated responsibility. Generally a natural leader will show interest and willingness to step up to do the 'driving' and may already display an ability to communicate with, and lead others. Before any of this can be implemented, the transition is generally predicated on your having a firm and full grasp of the drivers role.

The transition process should not be attempted while you are still in the process of systematising your business. This should be completely designed, developed, implemented, measured and embedded, before you initiate the exit transition process. If there is too much turbulence in the business and you start a tactical withdrawal, your team may perceive this as abdicating your responsibilities and will not step into the gaps you leave for them. The main reason why promotion candidates will avoid stepping into a higher position in times of change or turbulence is generally because they will perceive a much higher risk to their careers, their job security and the repercussions for any failures or shortcomings.

It is best to gradually introduce parts of the drivers role to a keen understudy in a supported environment where they can access the main driver consistently for support, feedback and encouragement. Throwing someone in at the deep end and abandoning them is a sure way to engender poor performance, failure in the task, disillusionment and potentially losing a good staff member. Furthermore, if there is no guidance there can be no corrective action and therefore no measured improvement. It is far better to have a phased learning program where one task or role at a time is mastered.

One of the most under-stated and under-diagnosed problems with the transition process, is the lack of management skills that any one delegate or candidate may have. One can never assume that because a sales person is the highest-achieving sales person in the team that he or she would automatically make a good sales manager. This is the most common mistake made by larger corporate and government departments, more recognised as "promoting a person beyond their level of competency".

This does not have to result in failure, but a good manager should ensure that if a candidate is finding difficulty in any particular area of their increased role, they should be given access to training, counselling and mentoring, to ensure that these skills are learned and embedded. Regular mentoring meetings will help to encourage these candidates to identify their weaknesses and ask for help when they need it.

In our Formula 1 Coaching Program, we set objectives with the business owners and this becomes their contract with us. They are firstly presented with a choice of three options and are asked to select which of these are more important to them (on a scale of 1-10) to determine what they need to "trade-off" in order to meet their personal objectives. The three semi-exclusive options are (1) Working less in the business, (2) Earning more in the business and/or (3) Increasing the value of the business for a pending sale. In this chapter, we will focus on the first option as dominant and will look to others in later chapters.

The first stage of working less in the business is for the driver to set a first-stage date to transition from 5 days per week, to 4 days. At that point, we allow these owners to operate ON the business for the 5th day, but not IN the business. For the first month of this transition, they may still attend the office, but are not allowed to perform any operational tasks. Our focus during this time is to ensure the delegation is optimised and that the work not done on the 5th day is not piled up for the first day of the following week.

The second stage of this process is to increase the depth of delegation and ensure these tasks are completed, with satisfactory outcomes. About this time, we see owners starting to miss the operational role and sometimes the interaction with customers, but we have to keep them to their plan, ensuring a reduction in operations and a shift to strategic functions.

The first step in the staged exit is to inform the staff as a group. You need to liken the planned structure to a large corporate operation (which should be your vision anyway) and you are starting the process now, so the staff can start to take on the additional roles and grow into their new responsibilities. Be aware, some will seek to avoid these additional responsibilities, but you should remain firm on what is expected and document the new roles carefully and concisely.

When you start to scale back your time in the business, firstly from five days to four days per week, you should think foremost of your core objective that on the day of your return you should not have to do any 'catch up' work. If you spend your first day back doing 'catch-up' work it means that your delegation of duties has failed and you are simply stacking five days into four. If you do not have to do any 'catch up' work it means that the delegation program is working and that you can gradually increase the number and importance of tasks to your understudy driver.

One of the most fundamental problems we encounter in the first phases of delegation, is the insistence of some business owners to have the delegates (the substitute drivers) perform the task to the same standard as the principal. One critical adjustment that needs to be made up-front (and accepted unconditionally) is that if others perform to a standard that is 80% of the principals' standards, the principals need to accept that this is sufficient. Not every employee or manager will be as efficient or as effective in their delegation of duties, as the principal of a business – get over it.

The succession process is all dependent on giving some real thought as to what you can delegate from early on without too much disruption, and building the confidence, ability and skill-set of your understudy with a well-structured plan to take up driver responsibilities. When four days per week is working to an acceptable and reliable standard, then it becomes an essential process to scale back to three days per week and so on. In time, your role becomes more 'trainer' and 'mentor' rather than senior driver and allows you to focus on the owner role and enjoy your life, or alternatively you can set about building the next business.

In a Formula 1 racing team, the driver is generally the most prominent person in the media. He can be the star. However, it makes logical sense that if he is the star and not the owner, he is generally not the most amply rewarded person in the team. This would be reserved for the manager, and/or the owner. As with any other business, this key person might be paid very well, given the skills and the prominence of their profile but as it is in business, it should not be difficult to replace any driver in any team, whether they are on the winning dais in every race or not.

Sometimes we may develop or inherit staff who believe that they are critical to the survival of the business and if unchecked, will start to change the operational process or deviate from your success formula. This will need to be dealt with as early as possible. In my 30 years in business and management, I have never seen one critical position that could not be replaced, including some held by myself.

These egos can be managed subtly, by simply implementing a layer of accountability (KPIs etc.) under the job description and integrating these with the organisation chart. For small business owners, this becomes less of an issue or a priority, but the perception could not be further from the reality. If you do not have a structure for all roles and their relationships to other roles (no matter how many of these hats you wear at present) you will not be in a position to pass these roles on to other people.

Every big business started out small, but all of them grew eventually. There would not be too many cases of a public company still managed by the same person who founded it, with that person handling all of the major business management roles, such as product development, production, sales, administration, as well as finance and accounting. Delegation is a critical catalyst to growth and needs to be mastered before the recruitment process. If not, the business owner will end up pushing aside the workers because of his perception that the job is not being done well enough.

Working your way out of the business should be your objective, after all the business is there to serve your life; you are not there to serve your business. Employing the disciplines of a supported and controlled delegation espoused in this chapter is not only the key to your time freedom but also to a greater business value when the critical time to exit nears. Just as at the auto racetrack, the driver may get the applause but the owner takes the cash. Wouldn't you ultimately rather take the cash?

The Transition

Most business owners will only seriously contemplate an exit from their business under special circumstances, such as health, disputes, family/ owner conflict, or the business runs out of money and can no longer pay the salaries for all personnel. If you don't get serious about getting out of your business, there is a very high probability that you don't actually own a business, you own a job. If business owners can set their egos aside, there are very few businesses that rely on key personnel and in those businesses, there is no value. So to consider your business as an asset beyond your involvement, you need to plan to operate it independently of you.

In a past chapter, we provided the analogy of Apple Computers and the share price reaction (over 12 months) after Steve Jobs stepped down, and later tragically died. The business proved it was not dependent upon Steve Jobs to grow and in fact released two major products within those 12 months, propelling the share price to nearly double that at Steve's retirement in August, 2011.

The most effective method of getting out is to plan the transition, set agreed dates and milestones and make sure that everybody agrees to these. Clearly there will be a void to fill in any company that loses its senior manager, but you may be very surprised at how well the people you have selected are able to step up and fill this void. If Steve Jobs can step back and barely create a ripple, you should not expect any less of your business. To transition effectively, you will need a structured plan. We find the most effective process is to start with is the 4-day week. Three things need to happen to make this effective.

The first change is that you need to be banned from being in your office after hours and at weekends. There should be no compromise on this point. If the presidents of the world's largest companies can do it, so can you. If your business cannot operate without you, then you do not have a business, you have a job.

The second change is that you need to schedule one day (the same day every week) that you will not be attending the office. This should be promoted in advance and staff should be instructed that they are not to ring you with problems, but need to take initiative and authority and deal with whatever comes up. If they can't deal with it, they should re-schedule the issue for the next working day, but not call you.

The third change is to get a commitment from everyone in your team (and yourself) that you are not going to have to deal with the 5th day's work on your first day back. This has to be stated publically to all team members and is best written up on your office wall, to ensure that everybody is reminded of this. In many cases, this becomes the weak link in the transition function chain. With proper planning, assertive direction and strong corrective action on any breaches, you will be able to embed this within 3-4 weeks.

Once you have the four-day week, you will have to become proficient at monitoring the business from a distance (perhaps the golf course) and you will start to become adept at using the monitoring tools we have provided in earlier chapters. After three weeks, your new process will become a habit, for you and for your team.

The next step is to take leave. You need to schedule at least 2 weeks where you will not come into the office, but you will require daily dashboard reporting by your senior manager(s) which will allow you to assess and track the business activity over this 2 weeks. It is generally preferred for you to be out of town and for at least two weeks, but 4 weeks is more desirable.

Once your team falls into the "Friday" routine of working without the boss, they will either step up or slack off. This should not be a collective response, but an individual response for each team member. This will be the only way for you (without CCTV cameras) to determine who actually works and who just collects a pay packet each week. If the entire team slacks off, there will almost certainly be a major issue in the business culture, which you will need to address immediately.

Whilst we all fear this may happen in our business, it rarely does. The only direct way to determine if it will, is to step out for these weeks and to monitor the metrics that your business should use, to determine that the levels of quality activity and achievement are present.

The final phase of transitioning yourself out is to call a group meeting, preferably over a lunch or after hours relaxation time, and point out to everybody, that "…although the company is doing OK, I have decided to fire someone…, me." It is best to explain carefully that they were recruited and trained to run their sections as managers and now you have the trust in all of them to not just maintain the business activity as it is, but add their personality and flair (without risking the business) and to grow the company at the same or at a greater rate, than it has been under your guidance.

This is the most appropriate moment to share the forward growth, with equity, options or other earned-in bonuses, for exceptional performance, long service and other achievements.

SUMMARY POINTS

☑ Business owner transition is by far the most difficult task of the consultant or coach. The only genuine impediment in nearly all cases is between the ears of the business owner.

☑ As consultants, we start to work on the mindset shift very early in the change process, as we have to overcome a lot of embedded beliefs about the necessity of the business owner's contribution.

☑ The first stage is to have the owner make a commitment to a 4-day week and plan how this will take effect.

☑ The second stage is to measure the results and identify if this business owner is delegating or not, which will manifest itself if the owner is doing the extra work on their next day back.

☑ The third stage is to take between two and 6 weeks off (usually a holiday) and we establish the KPIs this owner will monitor, as the staff start to manage themselves and their respective subordinates.

☑ On returning to the workplace, the business owner is usually shocked to learn that business continued in their absence. This is the second critical turning point and we use this to reduce the business owner's involvement permanently and we hand them the role of consultant. They have the KPIs and other metrics to measure and they only ask questions or seek explanations when some of the metrics are outside the acceptable limits.

CHAPTER 10

Getting to Pole Position – Grooming the Business for Sale

"It's far better to buy a wonderful company at a fair price than a fair company at a wonderful price."

Warren Buffet

CHAPTER 10

GETTING TO POLE POSITION – GROOMING THE BUSINESS FOR SALE

As a child (and well into my adult years) I enjoyed playing the game of monopoly. I liked to collect whatever I could (even if I didn't want it) knowing that at some point I could trade the streets I didn't want, for much more than their stated value. This lesson in leveraged value is critical for every business owner, as it serves to show that some assets are strategically or tactically more valuable to some buyers. Also, if the game was played right, you had more sources of income to build your wealth. Sadly, the real estate market in most countries has taken a severe and painful correction in recent years, providing far less opportunity for these assets to provide a source of income beyond their cost.

This is where businesses will shine. In most cases, a business should return at least half the purchase price every year and properly managed, can out-perform the real estate market or CPI. There are additional risks associated with owning a portfolio of businesses, but these can be easily managed with the proper goals, procedures, measurables and controls. This could suggest that if you were able to aggregate several or many businesses into a single portfolio, you might outperform a portfolio of residential or even commercial properties.

This is what the stock market does every day. Most industries have many businesses (sometimes referred to a divisions) – related or un-related, which collectively provide a return to shareholders well above property portfolios. The key to making this sustainable is to (1) Have professional systems and management in place – and this book is your first step to having both, (2) To have an asset that, with your skills, can be grown far more rapidly than any static or generic investment, and (3) To have an exit for each business; to a willing buyer who can afford to pay a premium.

The core objective of this book is to have you view your business skills as the real asset and to deploy those skills in building a portfolio of business assets that out-perform their competitors and can be sought after by corporate buyers for a higher multiplier (as is the case with public companies paying up to a 6-times multiplier for a scrip-for-scrip share swap).

Even if there is no objective to sell the business in the foreseeable future, the prudent thing to do from both an 'operational efficiency' and a 'profitability' perspective is to set the business up and run it with the objective of maximising the sale value of the business. This is because in pursuing maximum value for the business the owner along the way will secure other benefits associated with 'owning' a successful business such as personal financial freedom, time freedom and the lifestyle choices attached to these liberties.

Everyone in business should have as their greatest imperative to maximise the value of the business through continuous, profitable growth. If you are standing still you are actually going backwards.

Despite clear indicators that literally hundreds of thousands of businesses in Australia will be up for sale in the coming years, surveys have shown that the stated percentage of the businesses that have a well-defined exit plan is under 5%. This includes any ideas for potential exit that may be hand-written on a loose leaf sheet of paper. So, if you eliminated these, then the proportion of SME's which have an exit plan is even less. The tragic thing about this statistic is that when a business owner elects to sell his business, he does so without any real understanding of what makes a business valuable and most importantly, what a business buyer is prepared to pay when looking for a suitable business.

Typically, small to medium enterprises which have not undergone a specific and dedicated program to make the business 'sale-ready' will sell their business for a profit multiple of around 1.6. That means that after say fifteen years of the business owner slogging away believing that he is building value in the business with 'sweat equity', he receives the equivalent of 1.6 times his EBITDA (Earnings Before Interest, Tax, Depreciation and Amortisation). Of course he thought that his business was worth a million dollars; but if this business posts an annual EBITDA of $100,000pa in the most recent financial year - it may only be worth $160,000.

Worse than this, is the possibility that prospective buyers may not see value in the business for sale and the owner ends up closing the doors of his business without getting anything for it. The business brokers we deal with on a weekly basis all attest that this is not an uncommon outcome. It gets worse – you may still have a lease obligation and/or franchise fee commitments!

As much as the picture painted above may be interpreted as a bleak one for the prospect of selling your business for a huge payday, the reality is that there are always hungry buyers for good businesses - irrespective of where we might be in the economic cycle. The operative word here is 'good' businesses though. So what makes a 'good' business? Is it a business that buyers will pay a good price for? We will get to that shortly but firstly let's look at how businesses are valued.

How Your Business will be Valued

There are many ways to calculate the value of a business. It can seem as much an art as a science and ultimately the value of a business is what a buyer is willing to pay. However, it is valuable to know the basis upon which your business will be valued by the various players in a potential transaction.

The Asset Valuation method is used only when dealing with an underperforming business where the value of the assets themselves is worth more that the business as a going concern. You don't want to be in this category. If you find that business brokers want to value your business in this way, you are better off focusing on other chapters in this book and improving the business performance and profitability before returning to the market.

The Discounted Net Cash Flow method (sometimes referred to at the NPV method) is preferred by the large accounting firms, and is potentially one of the best valuation methods although it is generally not applicable to small and medium sized businesses. It attempts to put a value, in today's terms, on future cash flows in a business. This method is based on the concept that the value of a business depends on the future net cash flow of the business discounted back to present value at an appropriate discount rate.

This is a good method when future cash flows are predictable to a good level of accuracy as in the case of mining companies or large stable companies. It is less applicable for smaller companies on the basis that their future revenue stream is far less predictable unless of course the business in question has long term contracts in place and has a long history of regular cash flow.

More typically for smaller businesses (valued at below $3 million) valuation is derived through determining the EBITDA (Earnings Before Interest Tax Depreciation and Amortisation) and applying a risk factor to arrive at a multiple on profit. The EBITDA is divided by the risk factor in order to determine a valuation though an appropriate profit multiple for the business. The higher the risk factor the lower the profit multiple and vice versa:

$$\text{EBITDA / Risk Factor} = \text{Value}$$

So:

> If EBITDA is $100,000 and risk factor is 50%;
> then value is $200,000 (profit multiple = 2)
>
> If EBITDA is $100,000 and risk factor is 25%;
> then value is $400,000 (profit multiple = 4)
>
> If EBITDA is $100,000 and risk factor is 75%;
> then value is $133,333 (profit multiple = 1.33)

EDITDA can be slightly more ambiguous than you might think at first based on the fact that it is often adjusted by business brokers and accountants to reflect a valuation in line with 'maintainable profit.' 'Adjustments' (also referred to as Add-Backs) may include things like subtracting non-recurring income such as apprentice subsidies and new ongoing costs (such as a new manager) and 'adding back' costs which will not occur in future (owners wages and benefit and cost of a sales manager who will not be replaced):

Example

	2011	2012
EBITDA	95,000	105,000
Apprentice Subsidy		(15,000)
New Manager Wage		(80,000)
Owners Wage & Benefits		145,000
Sales Manager Wage Adjustment		_ 60,000
Adjusted EBITDA		215,000

Some accountants don't include accounting fees in the P & L in the calculation of EBITDA; of course you would think these SHOULD be included. The broker and accountant are seeking to maximise the EBITDA of the business to achieve the highest value however it is essential to understand the 'add-backs' and 'take-aways' to ensure that they are justified and do make sense. Also worthy of note, it is typical that smaller business valuation will be based on the performance of the last financial year, rather than an average of 3 years (with consideration given to the trend upwards or downwards in profitability).

Once the adjusted EDITDA is calculated there will be a risk factor which is applied to determine the profit multiple and the value of the business. The profit multiple to be applied to value a business can vary from somewhere below two up to around six (sometimes higher) depending upon a number of factors, including:

- The total EBITDA figure (a business earning an EBITDA of $5 million will attract a higher multiple than a business earning EBITDA of $250,000)
- Sales and profit stability

- Potential growth

- The experience of management

- Barriers to entry

- Strength of market position

If you have a franchised business with a monopoly in a given geography (like a post office for example) the perceived risk on that is very low relative to say a lawn mowing round, when there will be a lower risk factor and a higher multiple. The assessment value is very much based on the perception of the risk and potential in the business - certainty of income stream, number of customers, the extent to which it is 'automated' or managed, customer loyalty, percentage of repeat customers, competition, exclusive supply arrangement, positioning, years established, growth potential and so on.

Now that we have the bare basics down regarding business valuation, we can revisit those important questions: What makes a good business? What will buyers pay more for? and, How do I make a business more valuable?

What Buyers will Pay More For – The 15 Value Pillars

Naturally, the first consideration when a buyer is assessing the relative value of a potential investment in a business is 'profitability.' Due diligence is conducted into the sale entity's accounts to verify the numbers presented in the financials by the seller and then there is a risk factor and profit multiple applied to the profit (EBITDA) to arrive at a value. There are different (established rules of thumb) multiples applied to companies according to their industry and according to the maturity of the business. There are also a number of key factors taken into consideration in deriving an appropriate risk factor and profit multiple.

Following are the fifteen key areas of enquiry the buyer will undertake which will determine the profit multiple applied and ultimately offer furnished. These are the key areas of consideration when answering the questions, 'What makes a good business?', 'What will buyers pay more for?' and 'How do I make a business more valuable?'

Is the business 'under management'/How systematised is it?

Business buyers are generally not seeking to work in the business and place far more value on a business which is already successfully 'under management,' that is where the owner does not work in the business. A business under management demands a greater level of systemisation by which all employees are fully aware of their roles and responsibilities, work processes are clearly identified and clear success factors for the business are measured and monitored.

A business under management may sell for fifty percent more (or even more) than a business which is not under management. And businesses which are not fully under management but where the owner spends 'less time' working in the business are valued more by potential buyers than businesses in which the owner works full time.

Customer List:

When assessing a sale entity's value a potential buyer will consider the company's client list to understand the size of the list, whether the customers are regular, 'repeat' customers, if they are loyal and if the client list is being used for regular communication to maximise selling opportunities.

If a sale entity has a loyal and diversified client base, even if opportunities for regular communication and increasing frequency and the size of sales are not being taken, the value of the offer may still be as much as twenty five percent greater. Businesses which are too-reliant upon a small number of customers represent a greater risk and therefore are not considered as good a prospect.

Intellectual Property:

A business has greater value attached to it if it has intellectual property ownership. The likes of patents protecting their innovation, copyright and trademarks provide protectable and unique differentiation and competitive advantage over competitors. Trade secrets, although not formally as protectable or valuable as patents and trademarks, still provide differentiation and therefore equate to a business being more valuable than if they did not exist.

Intellectual property can itself be formally valued by specialist companies. Companies who own a significant intellectual property portfolio can have the ability to raise capital and grow quickly.

Brand:

The 'brand' of a business or the public perception of the business is also an important consideration in the assessment of relative value. The development of 'branding' in business is a careful and strategic exercise which can have a significant impact on the success and value of a business.

Whether or not a business has a positive brand at the time of a potential sale will have an important impact on the buyer's assessment of what risk level and multiplier to apply to profits in calculating value. Although possibly a subjective contributor to potential value calculations, it is clear if the brand is held in either very high or very low regard.

The Numbers:

The financial performance trend of the selling entity is another important consideration in calculating a profit multiple. If the revenue, profitability and client numbers of the business for sale exhibit an upward trend over the preceding years then there will be a positive impact on saleability.

This upward trend indicates to the potential buyer that the business is on an incline rather than a decline. This would be a clear advantage to a buyer and accordingly value is greater. Also, as stated previously, a business with a larger EBITDA will attract a higher profit multiple than a business with a smaller EBITDA.

Property:

If the business for sale has property attached to it, this contributes positively to a greater profit multiple and valuation. Obviously property is a valuable asset in and of itself so in valuing business, property present in the deal adds significantly to the sale value.

The presence of property in a sale also avails the seller of the opportunity to keep the property while selling the business. This will provide an alternate pathway to ongoing passive income through a lease arrangement back to the buyer.

People:

Another important consideration in the assessment of valuation is the personnel. Are the staff difficult to find and are they specialists, or are staff low skilled and easy to find? A business which is not dependent on hard-to-find, specialised staff has advantages over a business in which staff are hard to find. A business like McDonalds is run primarily by low skilled fifteen year olds, so they are easy to find and that business can represent higher value (less problematic) to a potential buyer.

Another factor is whether the business has long-serving, loyal staff. A business with long serving staff is looked upon more favourably from a valuation perspective. A history of happy, productive staff is a very positive indicator.

Market Conditions:

Businesses in which the market is in 'incline' rather than 'decline' are more attractive. For example Kodak, which was dependent on outdated, even obsolete film technology with the arrival of the digital age, was definitely in a declining market (prior to bankruptcy). This does not make for a valuable business because the market for Kodak's product was virtually disappearing. Conversely, a business operating within a market undergoing development and growth is a more favourable proposition.

Competition:

The level of competition that exists for the selling entity is another key factor in the assessment of value. The fewer competitors there are and the greater the differentiation to existing competition, the greater the value for the business.

Even if it is a competitive market, a well differentiated product or service for which there are clear competitive advantages is a significant factor for which greater value will be attributed by potential buyers. A business which can clearly differentiate itself from the competition is a good business.

Exclusive Products/Territories/Agencies:

Businesses which hold exclusive products, territories or agencies have advantages in value on the basis that competition is limited. Therefore, a business which has the exclusive right to distribute products or deliver services to a given territory has a means by which to generate greater value within the sales process. This is effectively a natural protection mechanism and is therefore considered attractive to potential buyers.

Management, Financial Systems and QA Accreditation:

The extent to which management systems enable a business to function smoothly will assist a new owner in having confidence in a potential purchase. Well-established and functional management systems which clarify the operations of the business, lend greater value to the business from the viewpoint of the buyer.

Well-established financial systems and audited accounts also add to the confidence of a new owner when examining the validity of a business. Insight into the finances of a business is critical to measure and manage performance so strong financial systems and processes contribute to the value of a sale entity.

Similarly, QA accreditation adds weight to the credibility and efficiency of the business processes of the selling entity. The presence of these systems lends itself to a higher business value. Formal accreditation is looked upon more or less favourably according to the industry, however as a general rule the greater the systemisation, the less the risk and therefore the greater the value.

Debtors:

A business with up to date debtors and established systems for efficient debt collection is a more attractive proposition to a potential buyer. Conversely a business with debts outstanding beyond the 60-day mark is distinctly unattractive. A table of up to date debtors (including a history of current debtors) contributes to a greater business value.

Sales and Potential for Growth:

Businesses in which sales are growing steadily year-to-year, are more attractive and therefore more valuable. Moreover, up-front payment for sales and 'cash' sales make a business more attractive and valuable to a prospective buyer.

Potential for growth in sales is also an important consideration. This may be as a result of the market or more likely related to opportunities to more actively promote products or services to an existing customer base.

Barriers to Entry:

Organisations which operate within industries and markets for which there are significant barriers to entry are protected from new competition to some extent and can enjoy an advantage in having an unchallenged profit earning capacity. Where barriers to entry are lower, competitors can emerge frequently and from anywhere.

Greater value is generally attached to a business which operates in markets where barriers to entry are higher.

Buyers:

A business for which there are identifiable potential buyers, particularly larger corporate or publically-listed buyers, represents a greater opportunity to on-sell the business for a greater profit multiple and therefore is more valuable.

Many of these pillars of value represent opportunities for any business to improve, both from the perspective of improving profitability and owner benefit for the existing owner as a going concern and as means of making the business more attractive and valuable to a potential buyer.

One of the greatest means by which a small to medium enterprise may maximise their potential sale value and yet is frequently overlooked, is a strategic trade sale. This involves identifying a number of larger players within the seller's industry (or a related market) to whom it may be argued that there are strategic benefits to acquiring the sale entity. After having 'renovated' the business and made it 'sale-ready' by addressing the relevant factors identified above, these larger entities are approached and seeded with the idea of a potential acquisition and the value associated with taking that path. This is the beginning of a negotiation which may lead to a far greater outcome for the smaller sale entity's ownership.

The arguments presented to a potential buyer might include (1) Economies of scale; the acquiring company will not have additional overheads to service these additional customers, (2) New customers; the company extends its customer base wider, (3) Cross-selling and/or up-selling opportunities: where the business to be acquired could sell its (non-competing products) through the buyer's client base and vice-versa, and (4) There is a strategic fit between what the selling entity offers and what the potential buying entity does; for example, it may represent part of the supply chain which presently sits outside the buying entities control.

Public companies will typically pay a profit multiple far in excess of that generally offered by a private company or private individuals; often delivering a profit multiple in the neighbourhood of 6-8 (even up to 14 in some cases) to make a strategic acquisition which will serve to strengthen their long term, big-picture view. For this reason it is a wise strategy to consider potential buyers for a sale entity a long way out from engaging in any 'sale behaviour' to maximise the outcome for the sale entity's ownership.

Another significant advantage a trade sale (to a listed entity) might provide, may be the rollover relief provisions in the capital gains tax legislation, in Australia. You will need to consult a competent accountant for this advice, but there may be an opportunity for you to swap your shares in your company for shares in the buyer (listed) company, without any immediate tax issues.

As we stated earlier in this chapter, even if there is no immediate objective to sell the business, the smart thing to do from operational efficiency and profitability perspectives is to set the business up and run it with the objective of maximising the value of the business. Running the business from this perspective provides for so many more options in realising the value in the business. Go to work on 'pillars of value' which provide the foundation of attraction to the right buyers and you are positioning yourself to benefit from the value in your business.

SUMMARY POINTS

☑ Business value (from a buyers' perspective) is explained.

☑ A template for increasing business sale value for sellers is provided, based upon the 15 pillars of value.

☑ Several of these changes can provide a significant change in the valuation multiplier that can be applied to the business.

☑ Who you sell to can affect the offer price. If you are able to package your business for a large corporate or a publically-listed company, you can expect the sale price multiplier to be up to three times higher.

☑ Strategic thinking in the early stages of business ownership can provide a higher price and quicker exit, when the business owner decides to sell the business asset.

CHAPTER 11

Exit Lane – Your Succession Options

"Start with the End in Mind."

Stephen Covey

CHAPTER 11
EXIT LANE – YOUR SUCCESSION OPTIONS

In the first chapter we challenged you to rank the wealth priorities for you in your business. We asked you to choose a balance between higher sale price, not working in the business or an increase in the net earnings. This chapter is for those who specifically selected a higher price for their business, at sale. This does not preclude the others from benefiting from this chapter, but we caution you from creating too much turbulence in your business, by trying to make all three options happen concurrently.

Getting out of your business is one of the most critical events in your business life, but usually the one event we least plan for. Have you ever noticed that business-owners who have previously sold profitable businesses are able to get more for their next business nearly every time? The key reason for this is generally that they are starting with that end in mind. The key question we should be asking ourselves before we start out in or take over any business enterprise is, "How will I get out of this? How will I maximise the business value right when I need to sell?" The answer is simple. We have to plan our exit before we start, to get the most from any business. This includes when and to whom we intend to sell the business.

There are a significant number of options when it comes to planning the sale of your business. These options open out according to the type of business, its location, the customers or clients that is services and even the age of the business, the clients and the product (life-cycle) it is in. This chapter is an overview of the most attractive options for most small business owners, giving you the impetus to start your planning process for the big pay-day you would ultimately like to engineer.

For most small businesses (to $10m turnover, production, distribution, retail or service) the majority of prospective buyers will be people similar to you. They may be from senior or middle-management positions (as employees) business migrants or people who have just sold a small business and are looking for another.

These people will pay a fair price for a good business, but do not represent the buyer categories which could deliver a premium price for your business. This is all very well if you are prepared to accept an 'industry-average' price for what could be your largest asset. Why would you work so hard for your entire career, just to leave the sale of the asset to chance?

If we assume your business is in good shape and should command an above-average price, then you are better suited to an optimal purchase-price buyer profile, which can fit into one or more of the following six categories. There are always exceptions, but for those who do not know where to start, this is a good outline of your better options:

Staff, Family and Partners

Although largely overlooked by first-time vendors, your business is always going to be more attractive to those who know it intimately and also easier to finance if the same bank manager is used. The decision interval (time they take to decide) is usually far less when all of the business variables are known. In the 1980's an entrepreneurial business owner in Melbourne, who learned of his terminal illness on a Friday afternoon, decided on a Saturday morning, to sell his business as a going concern.

He sold it in 90 minutes, with his bank manager calling out to the business premises on a Saturday, to consummate the financial arrangements with the office manager, who (with his parents) financed his home to buy the business out-right. The reason this could happen so fast is because everybody involved in the transaction was intimate with the business.

Direct Competitors – Geographic or Demographic

This is the first area thought of by experienced business vendors and the last area considered by inexperienced vendors. There is the awkwardness of sharing your inside secrets with your competitor, but this is usually done after a deposit is received by the broker. With economies of scale, shared outlets and the chance to have one administration across two or more sites is a tempting opportunity to leverage.

In a case like this, there are generally different disclosure rules, with just a top-line let of numbering being presented, in the first instance. Then a set of questions is presented and responded to through the broker. Finally, if there is sufficient interest, a holding deposit is required (to a trust account) before due diligence is commenced.

Your Professional Service Providers

In most cases, the only party who should understand your business as well as you (after partners and family) would be your accountant. They have clients who are as successful as you have been and are always looking for opportunities. Who better to refer them to these but their accountant, who happens to be yours?

The broker who originally sold you this business, is the most experienced person in marketing your business, since you purchased it. He may be a specialist and can provide a sensible valuation for this, as well as having

a rolodex of willing buyers who may be seeking a business like yours or perhaps any business that could be as profitable or enjoyable to manage as yours is.

Your bank manager is also a good source of business buyers, having worked with owners of similar-sized companies in your area. Some of these will have reached the stages in their business where they may have closed out all of their debt and may be looking to acquire another business unit into which they can expand . Again, the decision interval for such an introduced buyer could be expected to be far less than the average vendor cycle.

National/Global Chain Competitors not Operating Locally

This category covers franchise operators and/or national chain operators who can use their buying power and branding, to immediately inject profitability into your store. When presented to a business like this, your accountant and/or broker should structure another set of ratios based on what they believe this store will be able to generate, given the economies of scale and zero marginal cost of promotion, with their existing advertising promotion this is just one more location.

Supply Chain Partners

Some vendors are reluctant to include their suppliers, strategic alliance partners or their core B2B markets, in their shortlist of prospective buyers. Your broker won't hesitate. These buyers tick more boxes in the buyer profile than most prospects and in some cases would be offended if you offered your business for sale without mentioning it to them.

Larger Corporate Aggregations as well as Listed or Pre-IPO M & As

There are three distinct segments of the larger corporate market. These are the public companies seeking to expand, the large private companies (or overseas companies) seeking a toehold into your geographic market, or the most ambitious buyers, a staged aggregation by yourself and a few other entities who wish to bundle your businesses together for a public listing. Each of these buyer segments will represent a higher sale price because they will invariably use their multipliers across your business and can afford to pay more for your business than a sole operator.

For example, a listed company may work on an EBITDA much higher than a private company, because their opportunity cost of capital is driven by the capital markets. Most industrial stocks trade at multipliers of between five and eight, with some industries (such as finance) running as high as fourteen.

Working your Industry Multiplier

In most cases, business brokers have various methods of valuation and if you understand their most common methods, you can build your operations model around the maximum industry multiplier for your business type, which will force them to value your business appropriately. To do this effectively, we must first understand how industry multipliers work and how business brokers use these as a common valuation method.

Let's look at the impact of selling your business. Let us use a small hairdressing salon example, to demonstrate the impact of tweaking the multipliers, on the selling price of a business. For most hair salons, the

prospective buyers will pay 50c in every gross dollar the business has made, taken as an average over its last 3 years.

Let us assume that after some timely advice from his business coach, the business owner starts to gather client data and makes a database of all of his clients. He may then use this data to create a newsletter and then offer hair and beauty products to his clients (endorsed by him). This constitutes a second income stream from the client base and in international studies, has proven to increase loyalty significantly.

Business value can immediately become $1.00 per gross dollar. The business owner can identify his clients independent of the business – they are no longer 'walk-ins.' Potential business buyers are now buying a list of clients they can communicate with, as well as an order book for hair services.

Our hairdresser then hires 2 additional skilled people to work alongside him, so he can work for only 5 hours a day – 4 days a week. His salon business value now becomes re-valued at $1.50 per gross dollar on all of their earnings (as the business is now partly under management).

He then sets up KPIs for the employees so that they can be measured (using metrics like client satisfaction, clients per hour, etc.) to incrementally improve their performance efficiency and effectiveness.

He then steps back by increasing their billable hours and reduces his time in the business – suddenly his business is now fully 'under management' and measurable, so business buyers will pay $2 per billable dollar. They can do this because their LENDERS KNOW THERE IS LESS RISK in this type of business. He is paying more for salaries, but he has freed his own time to earn money elsewhere.

He introduces other services (waxing, IPL, etc.) in which he increases his average sale value from $60 to $80 per visit – this will equate to a 25% increase on his $2.00 per gross dollar in business valuation.

To get the business to maximum sale value, he then uses his newsletter to offer specific waxing treatments as an incentive for clients. He offers packages of eyebrow and/or upper lip waxing to existing clients, after a certain number of weeks (between visits) to get clients to make their next appointment in say, 6 weeks instead of his average 8 weeks. This is a set campaign (email and post) from week 5 or 6, to encourage them to make an appointment and receive a small treatment or service if they book before a certain date (which is their week 7 of their visit cycle).

By reducing the time between visits, he has effectively increased the visit cycle by say, 25% average (8 week intervals to 6 week intervals) and so he is showing an increase in his turnover and therefore his gross profit (fixed costs haven't changed) is now increased by up to 33%.

If this salon operator had an average of 800 clients who visited six times a year and spent $80 each time, his gross dollar would have been around $480,000. With net earnings (after fixed costs – wages, rent, overheads, etc.) he would be earning approximately $100,000 and his sale price would start at $50,000.

Using our process, his gross dollar average (without the sale of any additional services, etc.) would be 800 x 6 x $80 = $384,000. Assuming average fixed costs of around $250,000 his gross profit should be around $134,000 if he is not working in the business and drawing salary.

Because he doesn't work in the business himself, he is now looking at a sale price (with database value) of $2.00 per gross dollar - $268,000. This process can take 2-3 years, but it just needs systems and structures

to make it happen. We have a program to make this happen in ten months, so it can be achieved and then embedded.

Yes, the business operator is taking home less money in the short run – he is paying employees and so he is only netting $12-$20 per client visit, but after 2 years he is still getting double his price in sale value.

Most importantly, he is not tied to his business anymore – he is free to earn money elsewhere, in another business or establishing another salon or franchise. Most importantly, he has achieved this by implementing minor tweaks in his business operations model, but he hasn't begun to target and shape the business sale to a specific buyer. In specific cases, some buyers could afford to pay a premium for this business because of their own circumstances, which may or may not relate to the vendor's business.

The Strategic Trade Sale

The single most beneficial sale option is the strategic trade sale. This is where you identify a larger company that operates in your demographic space, but is not represented in your geographic space. Alternatively, they may be of equal or greater size, but supply services or products that either complement yours or they are above or below you on the industry supply chain.

The first stage of a strategic trade sale (STS) is to identify the players and potential buyers. Business owners who have experience in selling businesses understand the importance of this stage and will generally plan this out before they make an offer to buy a particular business. If they start with a target STS, they would groom the business to emulate their target buyer in order to be able to offer a very smooth transition.

The next stage is the research. If this is a public company, you will need to download their accounts and reporting documents and calculate which acquisitions they have made in the past. Where they identify acquisitions, you can generally track back to the vendor and ring them. Most previous vendors would be happy to tell you how the buyer valued the business (the valuation methods used) and this gets you a starting price point for your negotiations. You should also find out who the vendor dealt with and which were more flexible and which were more rigid in their thinking.

Now you can build the business in the model of the STS target(s) and focus on growing all of your metrics to look as they should. This is not about window-dressing a poorly-performing business, but growing and monitoring a business along the same metrics the STS target(s) use in their business. If your business is not performing well, does not have consistent growth and profitability, your multipliers can be as high as you want, but the price will still be minimal.

Finally, when your business is the appropriate size for the buyer, you are ready for the approach. If you are targeting a public company, your first step should be to at least buy some of their shares. This gets you into their general meetings and buys you the right to get to introduce yourself to board members and also ask pertinent questions on expansion and acquisitions.

Once you have a face and they have met you, you can prepare a personal note to the target player within the company, for a meeting. In the meeting, you do not make a full-blown presentation on your proposal, but ask the person if you can have your broker talk with his people, on the potential of an acquisition. You might have some top-line metrics for him, to give him an understanding of your business. This might include:

- Years in business

- Years under your management

- Product/service types

- Turnover (3 years)

- Profit (3 years)

- Similarity to his business

- Target market

- Location(s)

- IP or other competitive advantages

- Assurance that you are realistic on price

Price would not be an issue at this time. This information should be discussed, but not handed over. There are NDA formalities and third-party agency protocols to be mindful of and this person may not be capable of making the decision. Your desired outcome is a personal introduction to the acquisition team, for your appointed broker.

After this, you can brief your broker and ensure the standard of documentation is appropriate for presentation to the STS team. You should review all documentation and you should insist on a professional quality standard. These people represent your business to others and they can do this well or poorly.

Finally, you will need to brief the broker on the type of multiplier you expect this company will be willing to agree to. This is based on their working costs, not yours, so they will be able to factor in their own economies of scale and if they offer you a six times multiplier, they may actually be presenting this to their board as a 3.5 times multiplier, with additional opportunities of other products or services they could offer to your customers.

Transitioning Ownership

One of the most effective ways of obtaining top dollar for your business is to effect a transition sale with a vender-finance component on the tail-end. This is most favoured by professional and service-based businesses, which traditionally do not have a substantial multiplier. A good example of this was a retiring chiropractor who needed to get a top-dollar price for his business.

The brokers valued the business (after 44 years in practice) at $140,000 and he was devastated. We worked on a program to transition a suitable buyer, by offering the business in three tranches of $65,000. Before we commenced this program, we structured up a partnership agreement and a shareholders agreement for both of them to sign (after their legal representatives had reviewed this).

The first of these was financed by the buyer, from a second mortgage on his home. He immediately started working in the business and the price was fixed at that date, so that he had every incentive to grow the business before taking full control (he would not then pay for the additional goodwill).

The second tranche he funded out of his earnings, by setting aside 50% of his income for a 12-month period. He paid this off much sooner and then he entered into the third phase. This was a vendor-financed payment plan ($65,000 over 10 months) with both of the practitioners working in the business – drawing modest fees per patient visit. The vendor was an employee and charged his full rate for services per patient and patients had time to get used to the new owner and his methods.

The vendor finance offer was not without conditions. The buyer was not allowed to change the business until it was paid off (unless agreed to by the vendor) and if the buyer failed to pay the vendor each month (he had 14 days grace) the buyer would default on the loan and the entire business was to be returned to the vendor on a walk in-walk out basis. One of the key advantages a vendor has when offering finance is that he can set the conditions of this finance and in most cases, if there is any default, the business is not sold, but handed back to the vendor with forfeiture of monies paid. This is not limited to small business transactions, as Bond Corporations learned when they purchased Channel Nine from the Packer family for one billion dollars, under a partial vendor finance agreement.

Listing your Business

There are several stages to effectively listing your business for sale. These are best managed in sequence so that no step of the process can be overlooked or abandoned. If you are considering selling your business, it is important that you implement a process that will not overlook any of the important issues that could yield you a higher price for the right buyer.

Defining the Target Market

Buyers are always looking for cash flow, profits and the lure of improvement, in any business for sale. Where positive future trends are emerging, you can document these and use independent secondary research reports to support your observations. Some of these reports may be provided by the brokers as part of their engagement.

One of the most lucrative target markets will be a larger, preferably listed, company. If you are selling your business to somebody who is not in your business, they will typically be buying it as a sole source of income. This means they are afforded no more economies of scale than you are at present, if they buy. However, a larger, perhaps national company, would be able to reduce their operational costs and increase their buying power to justify a higher price.

If the target buyer is publically listed, they could be working on a gross profit multiplier of between 6 and 10, with some industries (finance, superannuation, resources, etc.) getting up to 14 times. Once you have identified the target companies, you can obtain their most recent accounts from the stock exchange and calculate their current multiplier and apply that to your business in a structured, formal offer. If you leave the economies of scale on the table for them as an unseen benefit, they will feel like they got a bargain and everybody will be happy.

Business Planning and Procedures

When you decide to sell your business, you should revisit your business plan so that any potential buyer can see there is a blueprint for the on-going success of the business. In most cases, buyers will pay a premium for certainty. It is also important that everybody in your business has a set of instructions they work to and that they can be measured by.

The buyer may have little or no understanding of your business operations and if presented with fully-documented procedures he will be able to understand everybody's roles and have a standard by which to measure each person. In most cases, including your exit plan (as you are now implementing it) will show buyers that you have adhered to your planning and are reaping the benefits of that.

Pay particular attention to cash flow within the business. There are several areas you can focus on that will immediately improve your cash

flow and make your business more attractive to prospective buyers. These include sales, credit control, good inventory management and measuring productivity.

If the business premises are leased, you may seek a written assurance from the landlord that the term can be extended (subject to negotiations) at the end of the current lease period. This can be difficult in major shopping centres, as most will not cooperate with vendors and can become quite hostile in the sales process.

In the documentation process, make sure you highlight your competitive advantages, your intellectual property, your exclusive and unique selling features and the level of loyalty you enjoy from your client list. Once a business is documented, some of the extraordinary and unimportant functions will start to emerge. These are the non-core functions that in most cases can be stopped or replaced. Nearly every business has these and most can function without them.

Getting your Accounts in Order

The business accounts are where most third-party assessments are made in the business sales process. If your business accounts are not in ship-shape condition and fully up-to-date, most savvy buyers and most accountants will discourage any prospective buyers from exploring further.

In some States, a business being sold for a price of $350,000 or less (excluding stock), must provide a Business Vendor Statement to a prospective purchaser (this is a reflection of the financials of the business, prepared by an accountant). In some cases, if a Business Vendor Statement is not provided, the purchaser may not be bound by the contract of sale. Some vendors decide that they will not prepare this statement until the business has a 'real buyer' at which point they approach their accountant to find that the lead time can be several weeks and during this time the prospect may find another business.

You should also get your accountant to brief you on the tax implications of the sale. In most cases, the way your sell the business and the time you sell the business can significantly affect the tax obligation. You should seek advice well before you offer the business for sale, so you can structure the sales agreement appropriately.

Once you have organised the financials, what about cleaning up the place? If you were selling your house, you would scrub and paint areas that needed it and your business might need the same attention. Sometimes little things such as uniforms, signwriting, and fresh paint on the doorway make such a difference, for staff and clients as well as prospective buyers.

Get Yourself a Broker

In most cases, a broker will perform a valuable function in representing you to prospective buyers, while you are actually working and earning money. If you are distracted by constant requests by different interested buyers, you may lose substantially more time than if you paid a broker, as the broker can field the questions with stock responses and buffer you from the endless bombardment of (sometimes insignificant) questions.

You should select your broker in the same way you select your selling agent for your home. This person must be experienced and knowledgeable in the business type and the geographic area. They must be able to provide a summary list of sellers for their last 5 properties, so you can call upon any 3 and ask about their performance. If they are reluctant to provide this, you would surely have to ask yourself why.

Fixing a Price Range

This process includes setting your asking price, your acceptable range and your walk-away point. If you set your range early, you will not lose money during the heat of the negotiations. It also serves to set the negotiations parameters (the acceptable range) that the broker can work within. If the broker knows you will not entertain a first-offer below a certain price, he will try harder to qualify the buyers, based on YOUR criteria.

Never leave it to the broker to set the price – make sure you select the optimal pricing method that best suits your business and will justify the acceptable price. Make sure your broker highlights the growth periods and areas within the business and the potential for more growth. Nobody will want to buy a business that they believe they cannot improve.

Make your own terms sheet – set the conditions you want included and the terms you will never accept. Have the broker understand your insistence on this. Make him earn his money.

Be wary of buyer conditions that could hurt your business. Some buyers will insist that you do not maintain your ideal inventory levels, so they can reduce the stock at purchase. Although this has an advantage for them at purchase, you will surely lose business as you reduce your inventories, as clients will not be able to obtain their ideal purchase item at the time they wish.

Finally, it makes sense to insist on reducing your exposure beyond the sale. This includes making sure you agree to only a very small retention. Make sure that all licensing, rights and obligations are transferred to the new owner and that your exposure ceases at settlement.

Set the Non-Compete Period

It is common to have a restriction on your ability to re-enter the industry within a geographic or demographic area. Include a clause that frees you from this if the buyer sells the business or ceases to trade in this area or in this business.

To summarise, the final payday for you is selling the business. This should be planned from the day you take it over or establish the business. We have shared many tips and secrets in how to set this up to give you a well-presented business to offer and we hope, like many of our clients, you will start to see the business and its potential in a new light and 'buy back' into the business before it is even offered for sale.

We find many of our clients fall in love with their business all over again, once all of the headaches are removed. Typically, they end up enjoying the management role just as intensely as they used to hate the operational role they fired themselves from.

When you decide to sell your business, how you present the business, the accounts and the preferred sales multiplier you seek will all work towards attracting the right buyer, through the right broker. When you start to tidy up the premises, you should also seek to tidy up the balance sheet, with aged inventories and bad debts dealt with before the accounts are formalised.

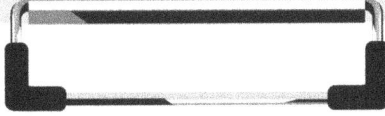

SUMMARY POINTS

☑ Most business owners consider strategic planning is for the operation of the business. Applying strategic planning to the exit, at the commencement of the business, is the most prudent practice for getting the highest price for your business.

☑ The six primary target buyer groups for most business are presented, to provide an explanation of the options.

☑ The process of strategic trade sale is explained. Business owners can elect to integrate their business into a listed entity and may be eligible for tax relief if they exchange shares in their company for shares in the listed company.

☑ The pre-sale process is provided. An explanation of the value of (good) brokers is presented. Terms sheets and sales memoranda are explained.

CHAPTER 12

The Championship – Setting up for the Biggest Payday

"To know is not enough, we must DO."

Leonardo DaVinci

CHAPTER 12
THE CHAMPIONSHIP – SETTING UP FOR THE BIGGEST PAYDAY

When Should you Prepare for the Sale?

One of the most frequently asked questions in our seminars on business improvement is, "When is the best time to think about selling my business?" This is a valid question for all businesses and the answer is always the same for all business owners. You should start planning the sale of the business before you start or buy the business. You need to have your strategic exit planned out well in advance, so that you maintain control of this as an asset and the business does not end up owning you at a later date.

You may have friends or know of business owners who appear to have the golden touch when it comes to getting offers on their business ventures, sometimes only a year or two into the business. Some common attributes shared by these types of business owners may include their design of the business around the sale, by structuring the business specifically for a certain type of buyer.

Some of the more successful small business operators can assess a poorly-performing business and determine how to transition this from what it presently is, to what it would need to become, to generate a far more substantial sale price. These strategic buyers are the business owners who know how to buy and then sell businesses and can walk into a business knowing who will buy it from them when they have the business operating at a higher performance level.

When you plan to offer your business for sale, you first must prepare yourself for pressure. This will come from the prospective buyers, the brokers, your family and even sometimes from yourself, once you find you start to adopt the 'it's time to sell' attitude. If you frame your sale decision as, 'I am not keen to sell, but I am open to the right offers,' you will immediately dissipate the pressure from brokers and buyers.

You may have known people who have sold their businesses without them having it on the market. They may have had a strategic buyer or broker walk in off the street and make them an offer that is above the general market value. Their preparation for this day, coupled with their, 'I could be open to the right offers,' attitude will provide a compelling invitation to the buyers, with no leverage on the pricing.

Understanding the Target Market

There are two general categories of buyers, financial and strategic. Financial buyers look for businesses they can buy in which they can finance 50% to 60% of the price and the earnings will have the cash flow required to repay that debt. These buyers will generally value a business by using a multiple 2-3 times earnings before interest and taxes (after making adjustments for expenses that would not continue for a new owner – known as add-backs). They deduct from the price any interest-bearing debt that they will assume.

In terms of preparation, there are disadvantages to selling to a financial buyer since financial buyers don't care about synergies or other intangibles, they tend to scrutinise financials to the max. Because they typically borrow money for a significant part of the purchase price, they are under pressure to increase the cash flow.

Most financial buyers prefer audited figures but in most cases it is not a requirement however, an offer to have the figures audited at their expense may be introduced as a negotiating point in the due diligence process.

Strategic buyers expect synergies with their other businesses (in other words, they think it is a great fit with the other parts of their business) or see opportunities they believe you haven't. They may sometimes be willing to pay a premium for a business but in most cases, they already know the industry and the market. This also makes them trickier to deal with because they may be able to use confidential information that you provide to compete against you.

If you would like to remain involved after the sale, be aware that strategic buyers may have plans for the company that differ greatly from yours. In most cases, you will not get your most ideal price from a strategic buyer, particularly if this buyer has had extensive experience in your industry. However, these buyers will generally make a quick decision and have a very sound understanding of what they can afford to pay for your business.

What Buyers Look For

When preparing your business for sale, it is important to align the offer with the buyers demand. This is not about what you like in your business, but what buyers are looking for. An experienced broker will be able to provide you with a very specific list of what will enhance your value and what will reduce it. Some factors that will make your business more attractive to buyers and potentially increase the sales multiplier that is leveraged on the business may include:

- Diversified product or service portfolio, with no one product providing more than 15-20% of sales revenues

- Capacity for the company to meet increased demand, with their current personnel, plant and/or equipment

- No pending legal actions or proposed changes in government regulations

- Financial ratios that are near or above industry averages

- Exclusive products, perhaps with strong branding or patent rights

- A diversified customer base – with no single customer making up more than 10% of your sales

- A strong management team (excluding the owners) with few key personnel, built-in accountabilities and performance tracking systems for everybody

- Weak competitors with a strong and growing market share for your company

- Products that are near the beginning of the Product Life Cycle

Some of the factors that could negatively affect your selling price would include:

- One single product making up more than 20% of your sales revenues

- Major investment required soon for plant and equipment

- Pending legal issues or proposed changes in government regulations

- Financial ratios that are below industry averages

- Generic 'me-too' products or services that are not differentiated in any way except price

- One or a few customers making up more than 25-30% of sales

- Strong competitors and/or a weak or declining market share for your company

- Products that are near the mature or decline phases of the Product Life Cycle

By using the above checklists, you can systematically work your way through your business to eliminate or overcome some of the perceived weaknesses and build on or accentuate some of the perceived strengths. These should then feature in your strategic business plan and your Business Information Memorandum, or Offer Document.

This document should set the tone for the entire sales process. It is not only the key to making a great first impression, but buyers will refer to this document throughout the selling process. It is your best chance to present your company in a most favourable position. A selling memorandum also saves you time and headaches by answering the questions buyers commonly ask. Adding independent research on the market (people who could buy from you) and the industry (people who could collectively sell to the market buyers) will show that you support your strategic position with independently validated facts.

The buyer is generally given the business information memorandum after they sign a confidentiality agreement, but prior to them meeting with you at your place of business. You can insist that this should only be given to qualified buyers since it will always contain confidential commercial and marketing information.

A good information memorandum must perform two (often conflicting) tasks. It must present completely factual information about your business, the industry and the market, while at the same time creating excitement about the business potential.

It is important to present the business like you would if you were raising capital or selling an equity parcel in your firm (generally you are – a 100% parcel!) in the information memorandum. With a prospectus or other offer documents, a public company always plays to their strengths and supports this with independent research and relevant photographs, to complete the picture for the readers.

In preparing a prospectus, there is an in-built safety process call due diligence, where an independent authority will review all of your claims and ensure you can support and validate everything that is stated. A private information memorandum does not have this due diligence process, so it will be up to you to always be careful that nothing that is included could be construed as misleading to buyers. Buyers aren't as afraid of risk as they are afraid of the unknown. Hiding the truth or using the information memorandum to mislead can be used against you long after the business is sold and settled.

An emerging trend is for inclusion of the IM onto a password-protected area on the company website, which buyers can refer to and refer their advisers to, so that less printing is required. This gives you an opportunity to have the website shout the same story and become a promotional tool to the business buyers, as well as your prospective customers and others.

Your Information Memorandum

This document must be a professional presentation of your past, present and future position for the business, with supporting facts and independent research validation (where possible). The framework for this document is fairly standard,

Executive Summary

A one page summary highlighting the most important points the buyer should know.

Company Overview

Entity status (incorporated company or business name) your reason for sale (very important), a brief history of the company and your period of ownership, an overview of the services and/or product lines with percentage sales of each line, and the core selling features that make up the reasons why the company is successful.

The Offer

You need to spell out what is being offered, does it include the premises? Does it have a database of clients? What is the value and age of the stock? What assets does it have? What licences come with it and what licences will be required to operate it in the future? This needs to also state the selling price and how this was calculated, as well as the required terms of settlement. Although you will need a little room to negotiate, listing a price substantially higher than you are willing to accept will not engage any buyers.

The Industry and the Market

Describe the market you service, including who buys from you (general descriptions – not specific companies or people) and a summary of who could buy from you but don't currently. If you know the current market share you enjoy, this should be stated (perhaps with a reference to the source). You should also describe the industry, including competitors and others who service the same client group. It is beneficial for you to describe the industry trends, changes in buying patterns, key buying preferences and the size and growth/contraction of the industry.

For products, describe each product line and its importance to sales and profits. Discuss competitive advantages, patents, trademarks licences and royalty arrangements. Outline the channels of distribution and how products are marketed. New products or services should be promoted in this section.

Key Personnel

This section should start with an organisational chart, as well as key personnel and their qualifications and experience. Photos work well here. If there are long-term contractors, they can be featured here and in the organisation chart. If there are union issues or past serious incidents, they should be mentioned. Job descriptions should be filed in the due diligence file, but not included in the IM.

Freehold Premises, Plant and Equipment

For buildings, a valuation should be stated, with the supporting documentation held in the due diligence file. For each non-current asset, you should include a description, function, age & condition, as well as location and fair market value. Include photos, drawings and/or valuations.

The Strategic Overview

This is generally a summary of your latest five-year plan, including objectives and an action plan outline for achieving these. You may refer to the business plan for a summary of the resources you have allocated to reach those objectives. It will pay to be realistic but optimistic.

Financial Information

This is the information you will need to have prepared by your accountant. This should include a short summary of at least the last 3 years of profit and loss statements, as well as a snapshot of the last three annual balance sheets. Providing a monthly or quarterly cash balance for the corresponding periods will enable the buyers to assess the financial resources required to operate the business.

Australian brokers have a practice they call add backs. This is where a substitute set of accounts can be prepared, based on a deduction of owner's expenses and other non-recurring costs or income. If there are substantial add-backs, a summary of these should be appended to the accounts. This section should also include sales projections, which can be tabled as a Statement of Source & Allocation of Funds (to allow debt and equity funds to be called to account in the trading statements).

The Due Diligence File

Some information memoranda includes appendices. It is our considered opinion that all appendices should be filed in the accountant's office, under a structured due diligence file. This information can be reviewed within your accountant's premises, but is not released to the prospective buyers in hard copy.

This contains copies of the company's product literature, detailed asset lists, valuations, photos, maps and drawings and anything else that would disrupt the reading flow if it was in the body of the book. A full set of accounts should be included here, and if an audit was undertaken, this should be included.

Once you have your business information memorandum set and bound up, you should then have your broker prepare a shortlist and a list of all prospective buyers to whom you would like to present this business opportunity. The top of this list should be publically-listed companies and then by opportunity. We have covered most of this in other chapters, so it will just be repetition if re-stated here.

Brokers are people and most people do not like to work a lot harder than they have to, for a small additional return. Therefore, getting you the minimum acceptable amount for your business will work for most brokers, but leave you disappointed. If your business is to be listed for say $2,000,000 and the broker has a 2.5% commission, he is only losing $5,000 if he agrees to write up an offer for $800,000. Under the basic tenants of negotiation (bracketing) the prospect of getting an offer up by 25% (from $800k to $1m) is minimal.

If the broker understands that you will not accept his discounting your business by agreeing to write up offers, then you will simply hold him to his contact and refuse to review any offers. If you are firm with your minimum price up front, you will hold a much stronger prospect of having this broker convince any prospective buyers it is not worth his while to draft an offer so low.

In conclusion, you must always remember that the business is not worth what it cost you to build it to what it is today (except to you of course). It is only worth what a willing buyer will pay for it. Sometimes this price can be much higher just by the way you prepare the business for sale and even higher if you target a buyer with a greater need for your business than others.

One critical factor in the sale of your business is emotion. Brokers know this and can smell desperation from the curb outside your business premises. You need to only deal with well-researched facts and be prepared (in your due diligence file) to back these up with independent sources that can be validated.

My final word on the sale process is for you to treat the business ownership as a game. If you have your business working very well, it is time to use your talents, knowledge and know-how, to build and sell the next business. Get top dollar for it and move on. Ultimately, as you sharpen the skills you have developed from absorbing the details in this book, you should be able to apply your business building and selling skills to any business in any industry. Just remember to change incrementally, measure everything, implement accountabilities, set up for the exit and make it ultimately run itself.

The Victory Lap

In writing this book our intention was to provide an appreciation of the greater possibilities which exist for smaller businesses and their owners. While it is great to learn new things and feel good about gaining further knowledge, we would ultimately prefer the book to be an impetus for action and be a force for good in changing lives for the better through more vibrant, successful business. To know and not to DO is really to not know at all. Knowledge is only power if it is put into action.

The fact that you made it to the finish line in our book, suggests that you are serious about transforming your business and your life and for that

we congratulate you. As Henry David Thoreau (19th century author) said, "Most men live lives of quiet desperation and go to the grave with the song still in them", reflecting what still applies today – that most struggle away in the shadows without the pluck and gumption to have a real go at their dreams. So we say 'seize the day,' 'take action,' 'be bold' and be rewarded for your commitment.

You are one of the courageous and privileged few who step up to the challenge of business ownership and have the opportunity to drive your business vehicle to 'your championship,' whatever end that is, be it executing a trade sale to a larger company, franchising your business or maintaining it as a successful going concern under management. Wealth and freedom for you and your family reside in the success of your business. Your success will require you to reach beyond your present boundaries and comfort zone, but the longer you wait to begin the journey the less likely you are to find that success. Act, but don't act without care and forethought.

Don't underestimate the significance of building your vision in pursuing your success. You must start with the end in mind and know where it is that you intend to go. Just the thought of an invigorating, rich vision of your future can be enough to fuel your energy, creativity and evolution towards it. The start of all great enterprises starts with a bold vision and yours should be no different.

Know where you are now before you plot where it is that you want to be. Understand your short, medium and long term strategic objectives and carefully craft your strategy to achieve your milestones. Ensure that you revisit your strategic plan regularly and make adjustments in accordance with the ongoing change in the conditions on the business racetrack. Make sure you reduce the weight by throwing out things that no longer help to achieve your new vision.

Measure and monitor everything which is relevant to the performance of your business vehicle in order that you can effect constant incremental improvements. Always remembering that, as with a high performance race car, there is no magic lever that transforms you from just another competitor to leading the race. Your primary competitor is always yourself and outstripping your previous personal best is the fundamental basis on which you will achieve greatness.

Aristotle said that, "We are what we repeatedly do; excellence then is not an act but a habit". Commit to outstripping your previous best by changing your habits, expanding your vision and playing a bigger, better game. We must take responsibility for our own destiny and as business owners we have the chance to take this opportunity, but only if we strive for greater levels of performance and that starts with our own habits. You as the owner of your business, will set the tone for its culture, the communication within, its performance, and the impact it has in the marketplace.

Change is inevitable and it is far better to engineer the change of your making rather than having it imposed on you. Take control of the change by making time for and dedicating yourself to the 'important' strategic matters which will advance you towards your vision while delegating the 'urgent' operational matters which will keep you in business bondage if you don't get away from them. Charles Darwin famously quoted, "It is not the strongest species that survive, nor the most intelligent but the most responsive to change". The success of your business – as with your life, is largely dependent on your ability to engineer your own change. Your business vehicle is not there to enslave you as the permanent driver. It is there to serve you in taking you past the chequered flags to your ideal life, but this demands change. Embrace the change, focus on the important and strategic things and watch your business vehicle accelerate.

Always remind yourself that time is our most precious resource, you can never claim it back after it has gone by. Unlike other resources (like money) it cannot be regained or replaced; once it is gone it is gone forever. However you can use it more wisely to build a better tomorrow. You should consider investing your time rather than spending it or worse still, wasting it. Again we congratulate you on investing your time in reading this book. However, we encourage you to further invest your time in applying and implementing what you have learned within these pages and to truly 'do' rather than just fleetingly 'know.'

With your business firmly under control, you have a powerful opportunity to engineer yourself and your family a better tomorrow. However, your business vehicle must be in premium shape, the driving of it must be top class and all the pieces of the picture for realising the championship value within it must be clear. We are confident that if you systematically apply the formula we have put forward you will be on your way to a profound and positive change in your business.

It is our sincere hope that by investing your valuable time in digesting the concepts and examples in this book, you have taken up the tools necessary to transform your business into a Formula 1 racing business, capable of taking you to your ultimate vision. In the future, if you feel that you need a pit stop in our team bay, you can access some of our resources on www.formula1forbusiness.com.

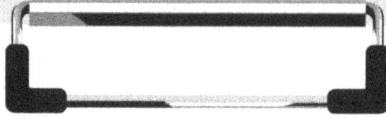

SUMMARY POINTS

☑ The value of timing for a business sale is explained. What the average inexperienced and experienced buyers are each looking for is also detailed, to help with the strategic planning process.

☑ A summary list of business features and functions that enhance value are provided, in the format required of the Information Memorandum.

☑ The due diligence process that will need to be performed by the brokers and later the prospective buyers.

☑ This can be a very intrusive process for the business owner, but is usually only performed under deposit conditions. You must be very sure this process will result in a desirable offer and insisting on a deposit before this, is an excellent qualifier.

☑ Action is the key to success – learning is not achieving, doing is.

APPENDIX A

The Due Diligence Process

Most due diligence is conducted by the buyer's accountant or an independent auditor, in the premises of the vendors' accountant. This is the last phase in the transaction, before settlement and hand-over. If buyers are going to make serious errors in judgment, it is generally because they do not conduct their due diligence according to a formal checklist. This process is critical if you wish to avoid legal or financial issues later on.

The Company

Results of a Google Search on the Business and the Principals

Certificates of Incorporation and Articles of Association

Any Trading Licences Memberships and Registrations

Board Minutes for the Past 12 Months

Organisation Chart – Job Descriptions and Payroll Summary

Copies of Agreements for Shares, Options, Voting Rights and Securities

Any Trading Names, Subsidiaries, Franchise Agreements or Restrictions to Trading

Financial Information

Audited or Independently Prepared Financial Statements for Three Years, together with the Accountants Reports

The Most Recent Part-Year Statements, with Comparable Statements for the Previous Year

The Company's Credit Report, if Available

Any Projections, Capital Budgets and Strategic Plans

Analyst Reports, if the Company is Listed

A Schedule of all Indebtedness and Contingent Liabilities

A Schedule of Inventory

A Schedule of Accounts Receivable

A Schedule of Accounts Payable

A Description of Depreciation and Amortisation Methods and Changes in Accounting Methods over the Past Five Years

Any Analysis of Fixed and Variable Expenses

Any Analysis of Gross Margins

The Company's General Ledger

A Description of the Company's Internal Control Procedures

Physical Assets

A Schedule of Fixed Assets and the Locations Thereof

All Leases or Loans

A Schedule of Sales and Purchases of Major Capital Equipment During the Last Three Years

Real Estate

A Schedule of the Company's Real Assets

Copies of all Real Estate Leases, Deeds, Mortgages, Title Policies, Surveys, Zoning Approvals, Variances or Use Permits

Intellectual Property

A Schedule of Patents and Provisional Patent Applications

A Schedule of Trademark and Trade Names

A Schedule of Copyrights

A Description of Important Technical Know-How

A Description of Methods Used to Protect Trade Secrets and Know-How

A Schedule and Copies of all Consulting Agreements, Agreements Regarding Inventions and Licenses or Assignments of Intellectual Property to or from the Company

Any Patent Clearance or Licence Documents

A Schedule and Summary of any Claims or Threatened Claims by or against the Company Regarding Intellectual Property

Employees and Employee Benefits

A List of Employees Including Positions, Current Salaries, Salaries and Bonuses Paid During the Last Three Years and Years of Service

All Employment, Consulting, Nondisclosure, Non-Solicitation or Noncompetition Agreements Between the Company and any of its Employees and Contractors

Resumes of Key Employees

The Company's Policy and Procedures Manual and a Schedule of all Employee Benefits and Holiday, Vacation and Sick Leave Policies

Copies of any Industrial Agreements, if any

A Description of all Employee Problems within the Last Three Years, Including Alleged Wrongful Termination, Harassment and Discrimination

A Description of any Labour Disputes, or Grievance Procedures Currently Pending or Settled Within the Last Three Years

A List and Description of Benefits of all Directors and Officers Insurance Policies

A Description of Worker's Compensation Claim History

Copies of all Grant Applications and a Schedule of Grants Thereunder

Licenses and Permits

Copies of any Government Licenses, Permits or Consents

Any Correspondence or Documents Relating to any Proceedings of any Regulatory Agency

Environmental Issues

Environmental Audits, if any, for each Property Leased by the Company

A Listing of Hazardous Substances used in the Company's Operations

A Description of the Company's Disposal Methods

A List of Environmental Permits and Licenses

Copies of all Correspondence, Notices and Files Related to EPA, State, or Local Regulatory Agencies

A List Identifying and Describing any Environmental Litigation or Investigations

A List Identifying and Describing any Contingent Environmental Liabilities or Continuing Indemnification Obligations

Taxes

Federal, State, Local and Foreign Income Tax Returns for the Last Three Years

States Payroll Tax Returns for the Last Three Years

Employment Tax Filings for the Last Three Years

A Schedule of all Subsidiary, Partnership, or Joint Venture Relationships and Obligations, with Copies of all Related Agreements

Finance

Copies of all Contracts between the Company and any Officers, Directors, 5-Percent Shareholders or Affiliates

All Loan Agreements, Bank Financing Arrangements, Line of Credit, or Promissory Notes to which The Company is a Party

All Security Agreements, Mortgages, Indentures, Collateral Pledges and Similar Agreements

All Guaranties to which the Company is a Party

Any Instalment Sale Agreements

Any Distribution Agreements, Sales Representative Agreements, Marketing Agreements, and Supply Agreements

Any Letters of Intent, Contracts, as well as any Mergers, Acquisitions, or Divestitures within the Last Five Years

Any Options and Stock Purchase Agreements involving interests in other Companies

The Company's Standard Quote, Purchase Order, Invoice and Warranty Forms

All Nondisclosure or Noncompetition Agreements to which the Company is a Party

All Other Material Contracts

Product or Service Lines

A List of all Existing Products or Services and Products or Services under Development

Copies of all Correspondence and Reports related to any Regulatory Approvals or Disapprovals of any Company's Products or Services

A Summary of all Complaints or Warranty Claims

A Summary of Results of all Tests, Evaluations, Studies, Surveys and other Data regarding existing Products or Services and Products or Services under Development

Customer Information

A Schedule of the Company's Top 10 Customers in terms of Sales and a Description of Sales over a Period of Two Years

Any Supply or Service Agreements

A Description or Copy of the Company's Purchasing Policies

A Description or Copy of the Company's Credit Policy

A Schedule of Work in Progress

A List and Explanation for any Major Customers lost over the Last Two Years

All Surveys and Market Research Reports relevant to the Company or its Products or Services

The Company's current Advertising Programs, Marketing Plans and Budgets and Printed Marketing Materials

A Description of the Company's Major Competitors

Litigation

A Schedule of all Pending Litigations

A Description of any Threatened Litigation

Copies of Insurance Policies possibly providing coverage of Pending or Threatened Litigation

Documents relating to any Injunctions, Consent Decrees or Settlements to which the Company is a Party

A List of Unsatisfied Judgments

Insurance Coverage

A Schedule and Copies of the Company's General Liability, Personal and Real Property, Product Liability, Directors and Officers, Worker's Compensation and other Insurance

A Schedule of the Company's Insurance Claims History for the Past Three Years

Professionals

A Schedule of all Law Firms, Accounting Firms, Consulting Firms and Similar Professionals engaged by the Company during the Past Five Years

Articles and Publicity

Copies of all Articles and Press Releases relating to the Company within the Past Three Years

ABOUT THE AUTHORS

Simon Frayne

Simon Frayne is a highly sought after business and management consultant, expert in creating business growth and profitability, experienced corporate manager, author, previous national level elite cricketer and an accomplished speaker on the national circuit.

Born in Sydney, Simon spent his formative years in Bunbury, Western Australia. A keen cricketer, Simon was selected for the Under 16 WA state cricket team at the tender age of 14. This started an elite cricketing career that spanned over 12 years. He first travelled Australia for two years playing in the Under 16 national tournament before travelling to England during his Year 12 studies to play.

With life still revolving around his cricket he juggled the demands of his sport and study completing Year 12 and then undertaking a commerce degree. He travelled the country playing cricket representing WA for four years in the WA Institute of Sport Under 23 team which he captained in the final year. It was during these years that his passion for individual and team performance developed.

Simon finished his commerce degree in 1991 and entered the workforce as an accountant. He went on to study the CPA (Certified Practicing Accountant) program and a post graduate Diploma of Finance, while still managing to play in the WA Sheffield Shield squad travelling the

country from 1991 to 1995. He also spent six months during this time living in England playing professional cricket.

In 1999, Simon moved to Sydney and entered the world of management consulting. His skill in strategy development, at mentoring and directing companies to achieve huge success rapidly became apparent so in 2005 he left his senior management role at Talent2 and started his own management consulting firm.

His company focused on pre-list capital raising for growth companies and improving business performance. Many of his clients realised huge success both financially, operationally and personally by implementing Simon's advice.

For two years Simon was the NSW distributor for SMI (Success Motivation International) and delivered phenomenally successful courses and instruction to individuals and businesses.

In 2009, he moved back to Western Australia and continued consulting to businesses both large and small across the country.

In 2011, Simon developed the Formula 1 program with associate Daniel O'Connor. The incredibly successful program helps businesses massively boost their success to reach their full potential, profitability and value while allowing owners to take back control of their lives.

Simon has travelled extensively both nationally and internationally. Just some of the countries he has visited or lived in include England, Scotland, United Arab Emirates, Indonesia and Thailand.

With a past as an elite sportsman, keeping in shape is important to Simon. He is a keen mountain biker and tennis player and loves his daily fitness training. He enjoys public speaking and is a frequently awarded speaker within Toastmasters International. He also enjoys reading and working on his personal development to craft a life of contribution, joy, achievement and adventure.

He lives in Bunbury, Western Australia with long term friend Skye and beloved boxer dog Farouk.

Daniel J. O'Connor
B.Bus, MBA, FAICD (Dip), AAMI, MAIM, CPM

Daniel O'Connor is a superstar of the international business world, a highly sought after Intellectual Property commercialisation specialist, a Master Coach, a company director, a business growth expert and author.

Daniel's skills are in demand across Australia and internationally in a range of specialist areas. He has spent 25 years in professional practice, specialising in Intellectual Property (IP) commercialisation – helping to get intellectual property into the market and achieve massive success.

Currently the Consultant Principal and majority shareholder in Xenex Group, Daniel has helped many companies to incredible international trading success with their concepts. He has assembled a team of highly skilled consultants so his business, which can service the needs of a huge range of clients.

Daniel has planned and managed public and private companies over his career with outstanding results.

A constant thirst for learning has seen Daniel study in Australia and internationally to acquire many qualifications including Bachelor of Business (Marketing) and an MBA in International Business, as well as being on his way to completing his PhD in International Business (Intellectual Property).

Daniel has helped boost companies to success through his knowledge, advice and mentoring not just in relation to their IP, but also strategic management, acquisitions, performance management, business systems and process improvements, interpersonal coaching and change management.

He has established new business ventures in engineering, e-commerce, knowledge management, automotive, agriculture and aquaculture, pharmacology, food tourism, microbiology, electrical and electronics as well as IT and education industries.

Daniel relaunched Success Motivation International (SMI) across Australia in 2006 after an 18 year absence. SMI is a franchised organisation of independent distributors dedicated to personal development through a specific goal setting process. Daniel worked with senior managers, business owners and executives with leadership and goal-setting programs to help them exponentially increase their success.

Over his career working internationally, Daniel has established firms in China and other emerging markets, as well as negotiating and establishing distribution networks for Australian firms throughout Asia and south east Asia.

As the first Master Coach for Western Australia with Maus Business Systems, Daniel has highly developed skills to help other people reach their goals – both personal and professional – in the shortest time possible. These skills have skyrocketed not only his own success, but that of countless others as well.

Daniel's extensive knowledge and network of contacts internationally means he can open doors to opportunities that others don't have access to. Throughout his career, he has enabled clients to raise millions of dollars in grants and investment and commercialisation funds.

Daniel has worked and studied extensively internationally over many years. His international experience includes many countries in Asia and south east Asia as well as the USA and Canada.

Daniel is a member, fellow or associate of numerous organisations, including the Australian Institute of Management, the Australian Institute of Company Directors, and the Australian Marketing Institute just to name a few.

He lives in Perth, Western Australia with his 7 year old son, Jaxon.

www.ingramcontent.com/pod-product-compliance
Lightning Source LLC
Chambersburg PA
CBHW060353200326
41519CB00011BA/2129